MYSTICISM
METAPHYSICS
AND
MARITAIN

BOOKS BY JAMES AND TYRA ARRAJ

MYSTICISM, METAPHYSICS AND MARITAIN

JUNGIAN AND CATHOLIC?

TRACKING THE ELUSIVE HUMAN
Volume I: A Practical Guide to
C.G. Jung's Psychological Types
W.H. Sheldon's Body and Temperament Types
and Their Integration

TRACKING THE ELUSIVE HUMAN
Volume II: An Advanced Guide to the Typological
Worlds of C.G. Jung, W.H. Sheldon, Their Integration
and the Biochemical Typology of the Future

ST. JOHN OF THE CROSS AND DR. C.G. JUNG
Christian Mysticism in the Light of
Jungian Psychology

A JUNGIAN PSYCHOLOGY RESOURCE GUIDE

THE INNER NATURE OF FAITH
A Mysterious Knowledge
Coming Through the Heart

GOD, ZEN AND THE INTUITION OF BEING

IS THERE A SOLUTION TO THE CATHOLIC
DEBATE ON CONTRACEPTION?

THE TREASURES OF SIMPLE LIVING
A Family's Search for a Simpler and More
Meaningful Life in the Middle of a Forest

ON THE ROAD TO
THE SPIRITUAL UNCONSCIOUS

MYSTICISM
METAPHYSICS
AND
MARITAIN

JAMES ARRAJ

INNER GROWTH BOOKS

B
2430
.M34
A77
1993

Vidimus et approbamus
ad normam Statutorum Universitatis

Romae, ex Pontificia Universitate Gregoriana

die 12, mensis martii, anni 1993

R.P.Prof. Charles A. Bernard, S.J.
R.P.Prof. John Navone, S.J.

For ordering information on this and other titles see the back pages or write:

Inner Growth Books and Videos
Box 520
Chiloquin, OR 97624

The author invites your comments through the above address.

This book is printed on acid free paper.

ISBN: 0-914073-07-9

To Jacques, Raissa and Vera

Good guides and good friends

TABLE OF CONTENTS

INTRODUCTION

The twentieth century has seen a remarkable renewal of interest in Christian mysticism. In its first decades the accent was on the rediscovery and development of a genuine theology of contemplation, while its closing years are seeing a widespread interest in the practice of contemplative prayer.

But much remains to be done. Theology and practice have not always gone hand in hand, to the impoverishment of both. Fine theoretical works appeared in the first half of the century, but they were often read in an atmosphere that said that any personal interest in mysticism was dangerous. Today, the situation has swung in the other direction. The enthusiastic practical interest in all things mystical is too often blind to what the theology and history of mysticism can tell it. What is needed is a bridge between theory and practice, theology and spirituality, and Jacques Maritain can help us construct it. In his work on mysticism we can find a deep grasp of the philosophical and theological foundations of mysticism united with a profound interest in the practice of the life of prayer which expressed itself most visibly in the contemplative vocation of his wife Raissa.

Although I am going to concentrate on Maritain's philosophical and theological treatment of contemplation, it cannot be done at the expense of separating it from the living context out of which it emerged and the ultimate goal it served without perpetuating the very split between theory and practice that we would like to heal.

In an essay entitled, "No Knowledge without Intuition" Jacques Maritain outlines the program that I would like to follow here. Writing of philosophical contemplation he says:

"Let us remark immediately that this philosophical contemplation has as neighbors two other sorts of contemplation - the contemplation proper to supernatural mysticism and the contemplation proper to natural mysticism - from which it is necessary to carefully distinguish it. These three types of contemplation are able, in fact, among this or that person to give rise to different mixtures. Of themselves and by essence they are totally different."

In Chapter I we will look at Maritain's philosophical contemplation, and how finely interwoven were his life and writings. Chapter II examines supernatural or mystical contemplation which is rooted in faith and is a knowledge that comes through love. Chapter III examines what Maritain called natural mysticism and which he felt held great promise for Christian dialogue with other religions. In Chapter IV we will see how Maritain integrates these different kinds of contemplation and situate his metaphysical and mystical thought in the framework of his time and the history of Thomism. Finally, in Chapter V we will look at what Maritain called the spiritual unconscious, the matrix in which these contemplations live, and an idea that could open the door to a deeper understanding of all of them.

I had looked forward to writing this book and to having the opportunity to immerse myself in Maritain's metaphysical and mystical writings which had been my companions for many years. But as I followed the development of his thought I noticed certain critical turning points which led me in a direction I had not anticipated. Maritain had worked on until his death at 90 years of age, and he said he was trying to open up new paths for those who would come after him. It was one of those paths that I came upon, one he called the spiritual unconscious, and which you will see emerge in the course of this book and hopefully gain some sense of the powerful possibilities it contains.

I owe a special debt of gratitude to Charles A. Bernard, S.J., for his constant support during the whole time that this book was being written.

CHAPTER I

PHILOSOPHICAL CONTEMPLATION

Jacques Maritain was one of the most creative and exciting Thomists to appear in the 700 years since the death of Thomas Aquinas. Today, interest in Maritain's work often centers on his social and political writings or the major role that he played in French Catholic intellectual life in the 1930's. But the Maritain of mysticism and metaphysics will prove to be equally if not more enduring. This is the Maritain, not of the past, but of the future.

Jacques Maritain was born in Paris on November 18, 1882. His father Paul was a lawyer and served as the secretary of the democratic statesman Jules Favre and married his daughter Genevieve. In the cultured and intellectual atmosphere of the Maritain home on rue de Rennes, formal religion played little role and its place was taken by the ideal of the service to mankind. Through the salons of his mother and his close boyhood friendship with Ernest Psichari, the grandson of Renan, Jacques had entrance to the higher levels of French intellectual society. But this favored environment did not speak to his deepest aspirations. By his year of philosophy at the Lycée Henri IV he was already tormented by his inability to find answers to the deeper questions of life.

In 1900 Maritain began studying philosophy and science at the Sorbonne. There he met Raissa Oumansoff, the daughter of Russian Jewish immigrants, and she shared his own burning desire to discover the meaning of life. In her high school years Raissa had thought: "...before all else, I had to make sure of the essential thing: the possession of the truth about God, about myself, and about the world." (2) It was her hope that studying science at the Sorbonne would provide answers to such questions, but it was really not science that she sought: "No,

I was truly seeking only that which I needed to justify
existence, that which should seem to me, myself, necessary in order that human life be not a thing absurd and
cruel. I needed the joy of understanding, the light of certitude, a rule of life based on faultless truth. Obviously,
with such leanings, I should first have gone to the philosophies. But no one had advised me to do this. And I
still believed that the natural sciences held the key to
all knowledge." (3)

But naturally the scientists of the Sorbonne would
have been bewildered by such expectations. When they
did philosophize they were drawn to mechanism, epiphe-
nomenism and determinism. If their scientific work itself
had to contain glimmers of metaphysical principles, these
reflections were far too weak to appease the hunger that
Jacques and Raissa felt. Raissa wrote of these days: "We
swam aimlessly in the waters of observations and experience like fish in the depths of the sea, without ever seeing the sun whose dim rays filtered down to us." (4)
Jacques, at least, could be partially sustained by his
interest in science, but Raissa, unable to articulate and
defend her deepest instincts, gave way to sadness and her
scientific studies suffered. (5)

They fared no better among the philosophers who
"despaired of **truth,** whose very name was unlovely to
them and could only be used between the quotation marks
of a disillusioned smile." (6) During his first year at the
Sorbonne, Jacques had become enamored with Spinoza but
found this philosophy "had no power to console the least
cry of a human being truly afflicted at heart." (7)

By the summer of 1901 they were close to despair.
Walking in the Jardin des Plantes they decided that if
life could offer them no answers then it was not worth
living and they would kill themselves. Yet the instinctive
workings of their minds, metaphysical and religious aspirations that had sprung up spontaneously in them and had
produced these questions that tormented their lives,
somehow still sustained them. They would continue
searching for a while longer. "...We persisted in **seeking
the truth - what truth?** - in continuing to bear within
ourselves the hope of the possibility of a full adherence
to a fullness of being." (8) They believed in the power
of the human intelligence to know the truth, but they had

no way to justify this belief, and this deep inner questioning had a strong metaphysical component.

As the new school year of 1901-1902 began, their des-
perate search was rewarded when Charles Peguy led them
across the street from the Sorbonne to the Collège de
France to hear Henri Bergson lecture, and in Bergson's
elegant lectures they heard the beginning of the message
they had been waiting for. When they listened to him
they understood him to say, as Raissa put it, "that we
could truly, absolutely, **know what is.**" That Bergson was
speaking not of the intelligence or reason, but a faculty
that he called intuition that was opposed to the intelligence and its concepts did not matter to them then, but
later it was to become a critical issue. No doubt they
were hearing words like the inspiring words that were to
fill Bergson's essay, "An Introduction to Metaphysics"
which was to appear in the **Revue de Métaphysique et
de Morale** in January of 1903: "...an absolute could only
be given in an **intuition,** whilst everything else falls
within the province of **analysis.** By intuition is meant the
kind of **intellectual sympathy** by which one places oneself
within an object in order to coincide with what is unique
in it and consequently inexpressible. (9) ...There is one
reality, at least, which we all seize from within, by
intuition and not by simple analysis. It is our own personality in its flowing through time - our self which en-
dures. (10) ...What is relative is the symbolic knowledge
by pre-existing concepts, which proceeds from the fixed
to the moving, and not the intuitive knowledge which
installs itself in that which is moving and adopts the very
life of things. This intuition attains the absolute." (11)

Jacques and Raissa attended a course in which Bergson commented on Plotinus, and Raissa writes of it, "One
summer day in the country, I was reading the **Enneads.**
I was sitting on my bed with the book on my knees;
reaching one of those numerous passages where Plotinus
speaks of the soul and of God, as much in the character
of a mystic as in that of a metaphysician ...a wave of
enthusiasm flooded my heart." (12)

Jacques and Raissa had become ardent Bergsonians
and the night of their despair pressed down on them less
strongly. They became engaged in 1902 and were married
on November 26, 1904. Later, in September of 1905 they

visited the cathedral at Chartres and soon after Raissa
was "on a journey and watching the forests glide by" her
car window when she had another of these deeply religious and metaphysical experiences. "I was looking out
of the window and thinking of nothing in particular. Suddenly a great change took place in me, as if from the
perception of the senses I had passed over to an entirely
inward perception. The passing trees suddenly had become
much larger than themselves, they assumed a dimension
prodigious for its depth. The whole forest seemed to be
speaking and to speak of Another, became a forest of
symbols, and seemed to have no other function than to
signify the Creator." (13)

These experiences of Raissa cannot be underestimated.
They were going to play a vital role in shaping Jacques'
metaphysical thought and he will come back to them
again and again.

At the beginning of 1906 Jacques had been working
on a Bergsonian essay called, "Preliminary Discourse on
Intelligence and Order" in which he describes his own experience of Bergson's duration: "As soon as leaving the
surface he penetrates in depth - reality, living and substantial, astonishes him and takes possession of him." And
he writes of an intuition of duration "...in which the instants do not follow one upon the other, which does not
at all admit of separated instants, but which completely
conserves itself in the powerful simplicity and the expansion of its inconceivable unity... he is in the presence,
not of an idea which seems true by its convenience, to
be handled in discourse and explication, but of the real
itself, which asserts itself royally, and makes itself known
by its force, through which it enraptures the mind, and
by its absolute nature, into which the most agile rapidi-
ties of thought hurl themselves in vain... Of this primary
intuition he will retain, when he had returned to consciousness, only a primary truth, and he says: I **exist in
an absolute manner,** that is to say, I perdure..." (14)

Many years later he commented, "...under the mask
of Bergsonian duration it was indeed the intuition of
being which preoccupied me from that moment. (And I
had already related it to the **intelligence.**)" (15) The many
implications of this fundamental text will only become
clear as we proceed, for example, the movement from

the concrete experience of duration to the intuition of being, and its relationship to the intellect, but we are witnessing here the decisive starting point of Maritain's thought, his own intuition of being which contains in embryo his whole metaphysics.

The next step in the Maritain's journey was something they never anticipated. They read a novel by Leon Bloy called, **The Woman Who Was Poor.** Bloy, with a gift for extravagant language, had the reputation of a literary brawler. But he was a fervent Catholic, albeit with the thunder of the Old Testament prophets and the essence of his message exerted a deep attraction on Jacques and Raissa: "There is only one sadness and that is not to be among the saints." Soon they were climbing the long staircases to Montmartre to visit Bloy and his family and he did not try to overwhelm with reasons in favor of his faith, but read to them from the saints and mystics, and their hearts were drawn even as their minds protested that conversion to Catholicism would be the end and even the antithesis of their scientific and philosophical studies. And it is entirely possible that their metaphysical experiences were playing an important role in preparing them for conversion by acting like a spontaneous and lived philosophical apologetics stirring the depths of the intelligence and better preparing it for what was to come. It was about this time that Jacques began to pray, "My God, if You exist, and if You are the truth, make me know it." (16)

Thus, under the influence of Bloy, their philosophical studies, and these metaphysical impulses a new world began to open up. "Little by little, the hierarchy of spiritual, intellectual, scientific values was revealed to us, and we began to understand that they could not be inimical to each other." (17) They began to think of faith as a kind of higher intuition but it was difficult for them to come to grips with its nature. If faith was beyond any certitude that could come from rational demonstration, how did assent to it come about?

In February of 1906, Raissa fell seriously ill, and they knew that their rational deliberations could take them no further. If only, they thought, Bloy could baptize them privately. They were still both attracted and repulsed, and Jacques said, "If it has pleased God to hide His truth in a dunghill that is where we shall go to find it." (18)

Finally they felt compelled to take the last step. They were baptized on June 11, 1906 and with their baptism their hesitations and doubts about their new-found faith disappeared. By now Jacques had completed his philosophical studies, but unsure of how compatible a normal academic career would be with his faith, he decided to continue his scientific studies. At the end of this summer of 1906 they left Paris for Heidelberg. Jacques had received a Micheonis fellowship to spend two years studying new developments in biology in Germany under the direction of Hans Driesch whose experiments with the embryos of sea urchins had led him to notions similar to the Aristotelian conception of form. Heidelberg became the novitiate for their little community which had now been increased to three by the arrival of Raissa's sister Vera. They devoted themselves to prayer and spiritual reading and a monastic-like schedule.

A month after their arrival Jacques was writing in his diary about the possibility of a "restitution of Reason, of which metaphysics is the essential and highest operation... We now know what we want and it is to philosophize truly." (19) Jacques' philosophical vocation that had seemed so threatened by baptism was attempting to re-assert itself, but the time was not ripe. He was fully occupied with his scientific studies and the nurturing of his faith, he was still a Bergsonian, and the inevitable question is going to slowly confront him: is this faith and even the metaphysics that he and Raissa have glimpsed in these flashes of metaphysical insight compatible with Bergson's philosophy? The answer was to come after a long struggle as Jacques trudged through the snows of Heidelberg.

"It was in 1908 while I was deliberating, in the country around Heidelberg, whether I could reconcile the Bergsonian critique of the concept and the formulas of revealed dogma, that the irreducible conflict between the 'conceptual' pronouncements of the religious faith which had recently opened up my eyes, and the philosophical doctrine for which I had conceived such a passion during my years as a student and to which I was indebted for being freed from materialistic idols, appeared to me as one of those only too certain facts which the soul, once it has begun to admit them, knows immediately it will never escape. The effort, unobstrusively pursued for months, to bring about a conciliation which was the supreme object of my desire ended abruptly in this unimpeachable conclusion. The choice had to be made, and obviously this choice could only be in favor of the Infallible, confessing therefore that all the philosophical toil which had been my delight was to be begun again. Since God gives us, in concepts and conceptual propositions... truths transcendent and inaccessible to our reason, the very truth of His divine life, that abyss which is His, it is because the concept is not a mere practical instrument incapable in itself of transmitting the real to our mind, whose only use is in the artificially breaking up the ineffable continuities, leaving the absolute to escape like water through a sieve." (20)

In short, this was a struggle to see whether it was possible to "harmonize Bergson's critique of the concept and the formulas of revealed dogma" or in other words to determine whether the split that Bergson had introduced between the concept and intuition could be accepted by someone for whom the mysteries of faith could be communicated in concepts. There was a philosophy that was growing inside of Jacques, born in his metaphysical insights and nourished by Bergson, and as much by the Bergson of intention as the Bergson of fact, and stimulated mightily by the philosophical positions implicit in his Catholic faith. "My philosphical reflection leaned upon the indestructible truth of objects presented by faith in order to restore the natural order of the intelligence to being, and to recoginize the ontological bearing of the work of reason. Thenceforth, in affirming to myself, without chicanery or diminution, the authentic value as reality of our human instruments of knowledge, I was already a Thomist without knowing it." (21)

We will completely misunderstand Maritain the metaphysician if we imagine that his Thomism came to him as a convenient philosophical appendix trailing in the wake of his Catholic faith. The actual situation was quite the opposite. He had gained no real knowledge of the Middle Ages and St. Thomas from the Sorbonne, or even from Bergson. Nor did he find any Thomism at the home of Leon Bloy, one of the most unphilosophical of minds, who had nothing good to say about philosophy, St. Thomas' or anyone else's. When we see Maritain struggling in Heidelberg, it is not a struggle between Bergsonian philosophy and Thomism, but between the philosophy he senses that is demanded by faith, but which he has not yet found. We are not dealing with a Thomist reactionary fighting a rearguard action against all modern philosophy and Bergson in particular, nor a convert who in his enthusiasm is confusing philosophy and faith, but a Thomist by inner inclination, a pre-Thomist who does not yet even know he is a Thomist. So he can conclude his reflections on these Heidelberg times: "When a few months later I came upon the **Summa theologica** its luminous flood was to find no opposing obstacles in me." (22) It was not some faded and tattered Thomism of the manuals that Maritain is going to discover but "an entirely new and correspondingly enthusiastic discovery of those famous routines still fresh with dew, and themselves newer even than the dawn." (23)

The Maritains returned to Paris in June of 1908. Jacques had decided not to teach philosophy in the French school system for fear it would compromise his Catholic faith and the philosophy that he was groping towards and so, instead, he found a job with the publishing house de Hatchette, first working for a year on an orthographic lexicon and then for three years, on a dictionary of the practical life. All this was highly uncongenial for him. He wrote of it in 1911: "Nourishment which insults the intellect and which it is necessary to vomit continually." But this work had one advantage. His philosophical understanding could proceed slowly and organically moving towards a lived appreciation of the basic questions without which any philosophical answer, no matter how correct in itself, is bereft of meaning.

The years in Heidelberg had been years of relative solitude in which the Maritains looked to God and the sacraments for the nourishment of their spiritual lives and had little contact with the clergy. When they returned to Paris in June of 1908 their life both in the world and the Church became more active. In October of 1909 they met the still unknown painter Georges Rouault at the home of the Bloys and it was conversations with Rouault that aided their reflections about the nature of art and later gave birth to **Art and Scholasticism.**

Not long after meeting Rouault their desire for spiritual direction brought them another important friendship with Humbert Clérissac, a Dominican priest and a well-trained Thomist who introduced them to Thomas Aquinas. Raissa began to read the **Summa** in the beginning of 1909, but Jacques was occupied with his work for de Hatchette and inwardly was not yet ready. He writes in his journal for March of 1910: "The dictionary overburdens me. I am enraged at not having time to study theology. But actually I am afraid of it. I am ensnared in my ratiocinations." But the light of faith had been slowly creating a new climate of soul in which a genuine metaphysics could grow. When Maritain finally read St. Thomas in September of 1910 there were no more obstacles to its light. The philosophy that had been growing in him all these years gave him the ability to penetrate beyond the externals of St. Thomas' scholastic format and recognize that his own embryonic philosophy was being fulfilled in St. Thomas'.

Even before he had begun to read the **Summa**, his conversations with Père Clérissac helped give birth to his first philosophical article, "La Science moderne et la raison" which appeared in the **Revue de Philosophie** in June of 1910. In the very beginning of this article the new Thomist makes his manifesto of independence from Bergson: "Reason is the faculty of the real; or more correctly, the faculty by which our spirit becomes adequate to the real and by which we know, in an analogical way, no doubt, and at a distance, the reality of realities, God. Reason is made for the truth, for possessing being." And he immediately makes it clear that reason in this sense is what the scholastics called the intellect or the intelligence or intuition, and it must be distinguished from reason understood as ratio. "...In as much as it is exercised by a progressive movement and uses these means to conquer intelligible being, our intelligence is called ratio, reason." And in an allusion to his old master he goes on, "In distinguishing in this way intelligence and reason, they are not distinguished as two different faculties, but as two diverse aspects - in reason of two different modes of operation - of a single and same human faculty." (24)

By the fall of 1912 Jacques could put away the dic-

tionary of the practical life, and having grounded himself
in the works of St. Thomas, start teaching philosophy. His
teaching career began at the Collège Stanislas and he
happily threw himself into the work. "He read a great
deal and meditated even more, and tried not to leave
unsolved any question dealt with in the course. Yet he
did not think he should give a ready-made solution to his
students; the solution should in each case emerge from
the discussion as a new discovery, and curiosity, the urge
to explore the unknown, should be constantly stimulated.
How tormenting it was suddenly to fall upon an unforseen
difficulty, and have to find the answer before the next
day's class! Jacques passed nights working on such
things." (25)

Jacques' "La Science moderne et la raison" was followed by a series of Bergsonian-oriented articles: "L'évolutionnisme de M. Bergson" (The evolutionary doctrine of
M. Bergson) in the **Revue de Philosophie** 1911; "Les deux
Bergsonismes" (The two Bergsonian philosophies), **Revue
Thomiste,** 1912; "L'intuition. Au sens de connaissance instinctive ou d'inclination" (Intuition. In the sense of instinctive knowledge or knowledge by inclination), **Revue
de Philosophie,** 1913. In April and May of 1913 he was
invited to give a series of lectures on Bergson at the Institut Catholique. These lectures, entitled "The Philosophy
of M. Bergson and Christian Philosophy" caused quite a
stir. "For the first time Thomistic thought was claiming
its rights in profane life and culture, entering the lists
with contemporary philosophies, entering into competition
with them on their own grounds, as young and even more
alive than the doctrines of the day." (26)

In October, 1913 Maritain's first book, **La philosophie
Bergsonienne** appeared. In it Maritain's decision of 1908
to break with Bergson's philosophy was worked out in
detail. He juxtaposes the thought of his old teacher with
that of his new and he tries to understand in a Thomistic
way the relationship between the concept and intuition
and the idea of knowledge by way of connaturality, and
it is Bergson's use of these ideas that must have given
Maritain the impetus to dig deeply into Thomist thought
and become the 20th century Thomist, par excellence, of
both intuition and connaturality. And Maritain is working
out, as well, the difference between what had initially

attracted him to Bergson and what Bergson actually said, or in other words, the distinction between a Bergsonian philosophy of intention and one of fact, and he had always attached himself much more to Bergson's inner tendencies and directions than to Bergson's explicit philosophy. "Consequently, by **duration** what will he understand if not **essence**? By **intuition** what, if not **perception of essence**?... Thus, by a strange effect of the intellect's instinct for self-preservation, the reader will involuntarily transpose Bergsonian theses into the rudiments of scholastic theses, and so will plant in his soul the first desires for the great Thomist light." (27)

For Maritain, Bergson's philosophy was born from a clear understanding of a cardinal error of modern philosophy which was the "perversion of an intellect which had been separated from its principles and given up to matter". (28) But Bergson, instead of rediscovering the true nature of the intellect, "abandoned intelligence and abandoned being, replacing the first by an extra-intellectual intuition and the second by movement". (29)

The hard won insights of Heidelberg made Maritain the defender of the intellect against any attempt to separate it on the one hand from its ability to see, to know, in short, from intellectus or intuition, and on the other hand, from anything that would sever this intellectual seeing from its means which are concepts and the use of reason. If we grasp this we can understand Maritain breaking with Bergson for whom, "philosophical intuition is sought outside of and above the normal functions of the intellect. It is called **super-intellectual intuition.**" (30) For Maritain, in contrast, "if we call intuition a direct knowledge of what is, there is indeed a philosophical intuition, but it is in the concept and by the concept..." (31) If we attempt to save human knowing by separating concept from intuition we have not definitively broken with the stream of modern philosophy flowing from Descartes because the original error of modern philosophy has not been laid bare. It is not the concept that we know directly and as an object, but it is the thing itself in and through the concept. The intellect cannot be rescued from materialism by a misplaced angelism. And this rediscovery of the concept had little to do with a textbook scholasticism which would be hard pressed to

understand the passion in Maritain's later description of
abstraction and the role the concept plays in knowledge.

"In the incomparable moments of **intellectual discovery,** in which capturing for the first time in the seemingly infinite breath of its possibilities of expansion a living
intelligible reality, we feel the spiritual word which renders it present to us well up and fasten itself in our very
core, we know what intuitive power of the intellect is
and that it exerts itself through concept... It is a question of calling forth a brand new Word, never yet conceived, from the dark yet fecund waters which have
poured into the soul through the sluice-gates of the
senses. Intellect gropes its way, strives, waits; it seeks
a gift which will come to it from its nature. It must
retain everything it knows, and forget what it knows
about the ideas that it has already learned (especially
philosophical ideas), plunge into a bath of active forget-
ting, render soluble and virtual and bring to a state of
confused vital tension its acquired experience, sympathize
with the real as it would in mimicking it. Beneath its
inner active light, at some unforseeable moment of decisive emotion, the coveted idea will be born." (32)

Maritain's words are ablaze with the joy and adventure
and sense of liberation he experienced in coming out of
the narrow confines of modern philosophy and discovering
that the human mind could truly know. It was this long
road of inner intellectual development, this road to his
Degrees of Knowledge, that was to teach him the nature,
limits and grades of this knowing, and he will always
champion the intellect against Descartes and his heirs for
misunderstanding the transparency of the concept to reality, and against men like Bergson who would rescue it
by dismembering it. In intuition, we have arrived at one
of Maritain's key ideas that can open up for us his
thought on the different kinds of contemplation. If it surfaced in his first uncompleted 1906 essay and his further
work on Bergsonian philosophy, it was to return over and
over again until "Pas de savoir sans intuitivité" (No understanding without intuition) which was one of his last works.

Maritain's intuition is his own creation which borrows
from the modern and general sense of intuition, is rooted
in the intuition of St. Thomas, and insists on the intuitivity of the intellect even when it works through con-

cepts. And the challenge that Maritain faces is to smoothly integrate all these elements. In the modern sense, intuition is a direct or immediate knowledge, a seeing. But it also has another allied meaning in which it signifies divination, a spontaneous knowledge that wells up in us without following the normal pathway of reasoning. And both these meanings were to become central in Maritain's thought. To them he adds a keen perception of the intellect as an intuitive faculty which directly perceives the intelligible object. While subjectively this knowledge takes place through the concept, objectively, the intellect becomes one with the thing known which exists in it, not as it exists in itself, but by "an intentional likeness, a sort of living reflection". But it is not this living reflection we know and then know the thing we wish to know, but rather "this likeness is **that through which** (or **in which**) knowledge takes place." (33)

Maritain is careful to place his more modern and flexible sense of intuition in the framework of St. Thomas' thought:

1. In an "absolutely restricted sense" intuition means, not a knowledge through a likeness, but a direct knowledge of the thing known which is in the subject by itself and as an intelligible in act. This kind of intuition is found in God's knowledge of Himself, the knowledge an angel has of itself and the beatific vision. "The intellect is informed 'immediately' by the essence or the substance of the thing known, **without the means of a subjective similitude of the thing...**" (34)

2. Then in a "less restricted but still strict sense" intuition means the sense perception of man and the knowledge of things by angels, both of which attain things as "physically present". (35)

3. In a broader sense, intuition is the knowledge we have of ourselves. This kind of intuition will become one of the foundations for Maritain's doctrine on natural mysticism. Here the intellect in the act of knowing something "perceives by a spontaneous reflection on its concrete and singular act the very existence of the soul that knows. This experimental knowledge indeed attains an object (the soul), **insofar as present itself and acting;** but as it apprehends only the existence and the action, and not the nature of that object, and thus remains essential-

ly obscure, the ancients refused to call it properly 'intuition'". (36)

4. Finally, in a very broad sense, we arrive at intuition in the sense of direct intellectual perception in and through the concept. Now while the intuition found in 3 and 4 are only improperly intuition in the classical sense, Maritain with a keen appreciation of Bergson is willing to extend the meaning of the word to include them. This gives us an insight into his way of marrying old and new. While rigorously adhering to St. Thomas he has his eye on the contemporary problems he wants to tackle.

Intuition is not opposed to discourse or ratio, for discourse starts from intuition and ends in intuition, for when all is said and done, the intellect is made to see. The intellect begins with being from which spring the first principles of identity and non-contradiction - "here we have perception without discourse, truly primary intuition" (37), and it ends in intuition in which it has reached "a conclusion, a final judgment to which discourse well conducted will have brought the evidence of first principles." (38)

Intuition as direct perception was to lead Maritain by way of the transparency of the concept to a deeper grasp of the primordial beginnings of metaphysics which he is here identifying with a knowledge of first principles. But the other major meaning of intuition, intuition as divinatory or as a knowledge by inclination or connaturality, was to be equally important to him. Intuition, in this sense, meant to know without reasoning, to make a correct judgment without discursive preparation, a more spontaneous exercise, not of any extra or infra-intellectual faculty, but of the intelligence itself. We know and truly know but not by means of discourse and reason. It is as if the light of the intellect, ever eager to illuminate and unleash the intelligible treasures of things, is not confined to abstracting ideas from sense perceptions and organizing them, but searches the senses and imagination, sense instinct or cogitative faculty and the workings of the will for new food to devour. The result is not demonstrative certitude but a more obscure yet very real intellectual knowledge that comes from reading the messages hidden in the very attraction and repulsion of the other faculties. This kind of knowledge will engage us a great

deal when we look at supernatural and natural mysticism
in the chapters to come.

In 1914 Jacques was given an honorary Roman doctorate and a teaching post at the Institut Catholique. During
World War I he was excused from active service because
of his health and redoubled his teaching efforts. The war
years saw the death of Père Clérissac, Péguy and Psichari, and its end brought an unexpected surprise. Jacques
had befriended a soldier, Pierre Villard, who had been
attracted to his work, and when Villard was killed in 1918
Maritain was astounded to find that the man he had
taken to be a poor soldier had left a considerable fortune
to be split between him and Charles Maurras. This unexpected windfall freed him from the necessity of depending on low-paid teaching positions to support his
family and gave him the time to devote to his philosophical work. His days of philosophical apprenticeship were
over and he was about to greatly increase his productivity. Raissa sums up this time: "The potentialities of his
future work were all there. But in order for them to take
shape and to be made explicit, much time, much experience and suffering were needed." (39)

These early years of conversion before the war had
not been without their problems. The Maritains possessed
that fervor of novices which has difficulty in distinguishing between the Church as the body of Christ and the
Church as a human institution with all its trappings and
weaknesses. Père Clérissac, for all his admirable qualities, differed markedly from the Maritains in temperament. He mistrusted what he called the reflex mind, and
unfortunately, tended to include under that heading the
contemplative spirituality of Teresa of Avila and John of
the Cross that Raissa felt drawn to. Further, he mingled
his spiritual counsel and solid Thomistic teaching with
conservative political opinions, perhaps not realizing how
difficult it would be for his new converts not to be inclined to accept his political views under a form of holy
obedience and docility. Clérissac's political opinions, Léon
Bloy's anti-democratic leanings and Pierre Villard's linking
Jacques with Charles Maurras, the head of the right-wing
Action Française, all conspired to put the Maritains in
a false position. They had no strongly formed political
opinions of their own for all their energies were engaged

in spiritual and philosophical activities, so they tended
to go along believing in a parallelism between the Thomistic renaissance and the politics of the right. It was only
when Rome condemned Action Française in 1926 were
they freed from this unexamined baggage and were compelled to try to elaborate a genuine social and political
philosophy in the light of the Gospel.

After the war the Maritains experienced a new sense
of freedom and maturity. These years saw the publication
of **Art and Scholasticism, Antimoderne,** a collection of
Jacques' earlier articles, and **Theonas,** inspired by Raissa's
new director Père Dehau. They began to have Sunday
gatherings at their home in the form of a Thomist study
circle, and these gatherings became a magnet for writers
and artists, philosophers and scientists, and people of all
different relgious creeds or none at all. Jacques' journal
entry for May 16, 1922 reads: "Talked at length with
Raissa. We have the impression that here we are the two
of us, in spite of ourselves, in high seas and forced to
judge by ourselves, as autonomous beings - it is just like
coming of age (I am 40! but 16 years only since our Baptism.)"

If it was critical for our understanding of Maritain to
see how he was a Thomist before he discovered St. Thomas, it is equally important we place his early Thomistic
work in the right context. The essays of **La Philosophie
Bergsonienne** and **Antimoderne** have a tone that Maritian
later regretted. Even in his first essay, "La Science moderne et la raison", which became the lead article of
Antimoderne, we read, for example: "The age has long
since come where reason perishes by the philosophers and
savants... and it is themselves, in truth, and the work of
their hands that they adore in adoring this imitation of
the intelligence, this pseudo-reason, perverted, unfaithful
to its Creator, despoiled of faith, sullied more and more
by inconceivable ignorance, denuded of all intuitive light,
delivered to the blind fantasies of a disordered reason.
(...dépouillée de la foi, souillée de plus en plus par une
inconcevable ignorance, dénuée de toute lumière intuitive,
livrée aux fantaises aveugles du raisonnement déréglé.")
(40)

Maritain regretted, not the content of this early work,
but its high-flown style - "It is no business of the philo-

sopher to have a style - it is not for him to give way
to his feelings." - and a language "so imperious and lacking in deference". But beyond that "I was not then aware
that if one can never be too right, it is nevertheless so
great a privilege, that it should always make one feel
apologetic... human truths require in the telling a voice
more modestly pitched." (41) But behind this language
that even a Bloy could and did applaud, there was a
passion that we need to grasp. Maritain is not antimoderne in a reactionary way, unappreciative of the modern
world, but rather he has suffered at the hands of the
wise of this world who could not give him or Raissa or
so many others the truth for which they were so desper-
ately seeking. There is nothing anti-intellectual in Maritain. The world of the Sorbonne was his world, the continuation of the world of his childhood, but this world had
disappointed him deeply. Maritain's attitude is different,
as well, from that of many Catholics who, having grown
up in the faith, look to science and contemporary philosophy as ways to enrich that faith. Their temptation is to
see Maritain as part of a defensive Church that fears to
reach out to the modern world. This is to completely
reverse the actual facts of the matter. The world of
science and philosophy was precisely Maritain's world and
one that he found lacking in certain basic respects. It is
one thing to look at this world from the point of view
of a secure Catholic faith feeling the pangs of its own
parochialism, and another to be wandering in this world
in darkness and close to despair looking for true bread
to eat. Maritain's early language is compounded of his
pain and joy of discovery and an inexperience that does
not yet allow him to always find the right tone.

This digression on Maritain helps to see how he could
write in his preface to **Antimoderne**, "That which I call
here antimoderne would be able to be called, as well,
ultramoderne." (42) When Maritain started teaching at the
Institut Catholique it was in the field of the history of
modern philosophy. But Maritain by inclination was not
an historian. He used history to lay bare the structural
faults in modern philosophy since Descartes and to try
to find a remedy for them by drawing on the principles
he found in St. Thomas.

For all his knowledge of St. Thomas and Thomas'
commentators, Maritain was not a Thomist historian
either. He wanted to free a genuine living philosophy
from the mistakes of the moderns and the worn-out
matrixes of the scholastics, and apply it to contemporary
issues. Already in January of 1920 in a lecture given at
Louvain, he could say, "Le Bergsonisme est entré dans
le musée des systèmes." (Bergsonian philosophy has entered into the museum of systems.) He had taken a sabbatical from the Institut Catholique during the school
year of 1918-1919 to work on an introduction to philosophy which had been requested by Church authorities and
which appeared in 1920. In 1922 we begin to see the first
signs of Maritain's own vigorous metaphysical approach
in his "Troisième cahier de Théonas: Connaissance de
l'être" which appeared in the **Revue Universelle.** It is in
this article that his preliminary remarks about the intuition of being as an understanding of first principles
achieve more elaborate development. "Philosophy is not
constructed... like a palace built in a void; it has to base
itself on facts, on the most simple and evident of facts."
(43) And what are the most evident and accessible of
these facts? "There are things that are." (44) (Il y a des
choses qui sont...) This primordial fact contains within
itself two affirmations. First, "All these things are." I
find in all of them a certain reality that I call being.
Secondly, "These things are different." And from these
two affirmations I see that the notion of being is applied
to all things and thus transcends all classes and categories. So I see that being is transcendent. Further, I see
that what makes things different from each other must
be being as well for "Things which are really different
are not able to differ by nothing." And if I use the same
name being for things which are essentially different and
these very differences are being then I arrive at the
analogy of being.

In this way Maritain begins to draw out the starting
point of a whole metaphysics from the mystery of being
contained in the fundamental fact: "All these things are."
He goes on to affirm that "being is the proper object of
the intellect and every thing is intelligible in the degree
that it is." (45) And once the intellect sees being it
immediately sees "every thing is that which it is and

being is not able to be non-being." (46) Maritain could
not help being fascinated by this primordial fact, "Things
are" which appears so simple and commonplace to us, yet
has hidden in it the entire mystery of being. Little by
little he will begin to reflect on why some people see
in this fact the inner mystery of being while others do
not. He is going to return again and again to scutinize
these metaphysical origins and to ponder the nature of
the special kind of seeing that allows us to glimpse the
metaphysical depths of things. But the next major stage
in the development of these themes is not going to
appear until 10 years later in Maritain's **Distinguish to
Unite** or **The Degrees of Knowledge.**

The Degrees of Knowledge is such an extraordinary
book that it will repay the effort to examine it in greater detail, for it forms the framework in which we can
situate Maritain's three contemplations. The structure of
this book is announced in its title which, according to its
author, "suffices to declare its plan and purpose" and its
external organization can be summarized like this:
Preface to the 1st French edition, June 11, 1932.

Chapter I, "The Majesty and Poverty of Metaphysics";
dedicated to Charles Du Bos. The chapter is based on the
material appearing in the Chroniques of **Roseau d'Or** of
December 1, 1925, which in turn is based on a conference
given at Geneva and the Sorbonne.

First Part: The Degrees of Rational Knowledge: Philosophy and Experimental Science

Chapter II, Philosophy and Experimental Science; based
on an article in "Cahiers de Philosophie de la Nature" in
Mélanges, May 1929, which is based on an article in
Revue de Philosophie, July-August 1926, which was based,
in turn, on a conference given on March 5, 1926 at the
Institut Catholique.

Chapter III, Critical Realism; two extracts appeared
in the beginning of 1932 in **Nova et Vetera** and the
Rivista di Filosophia Neo-Scholastica.

Chapter IV, Knowledge of Sensible Nature; outlined

with Chapter III and V in **Revue Thomiste, J**an.-Feb.
1931, which was based, in turn, on a lecture given at
King's College, University of London, March 19, 1930.

Chapter V, Metaphysical Knowledge; dedicated to
Raissa; extracts in **Vigile,** 1st cahier, 1931, and **Roseau
d'Or,** no. 46, 1931.

Second Part: The Degrees of Suprarational Knowledge

Chapter VI, Mystical Experience and Philosophy; dedicated to Garrigou-Lagrange; based on an article in **Revue
de Philosophie,** Nov.-Dec., 1926 which was based, in turn,
on a conference at the Institut Catholique, March 12, 1926
and at Aix-en-Provence, May 11, 1926, but leaving out
material on Blondel.

Chapter VII, Augustian Wisdom; based on an article
in **Revue de Philosophie,** July-Dec., 1930.

Chapter VIII, St. John of the Cross, Practioner of
Contemplation; based on an article in the Études Carmélitaines, April, 1931.

Chapter IX, Todo y Nada; dedicated to Charles Henrion, first version in **Vigile,** 1st cahier 1930; expanded
version in Études Carmélitaines, April, 1932. (47)

The **Degrees** represents not only a summation of Maritain's thought from 1925 to 1932, but the raising of this
thought to a higher intensity and maturity. 1924 had seen
the publication of **Réflexions sur l'intelligence et sur sa
vie propre,** (Reflections on the intelligence and its proper
life), but this had been a less comprehensive and more
historically oriented philosophical synthesis. If we look at
Maritain's previous mileposts in his philosophical development, that is, **La Philosophie Bergsonienne, Antimoderne,**
and **Réflexions** we see the long road he has traveled to
the **Degrees of Knowledge,** and how he has summed up
and transcended this previous work in this masterpiece.
And the **Degrees** is not only a summation of his own personal efforts, but of the remarkable interactions that had
been going on for many years in his teaching, the editor-

ship of various series of books, an enormous correspondence and the Thomist circle at Meudon which played an
important role in the French Catholic revival of the
1920's and 1930's. These study meetings were neither formal lectures nor free-floating discussions. Rather, great
philosophical and theological problems were presented,
usually by Jacques, and presented in all their technical
rigor together with a reading of some texts of St.
Thomas or passages from his famous commentator John
of St. Thomas. But the disputatios of the past underwent
a transformation as they emerged from the dust of history by being presented to a lively group of artists and
poets as well as philosophers and theologians. The volumi-
nous commentaries of a John of St. Thomas were to be
mined and their precious ore extracted from a historically
conditioned matrix, and "interminable controversies", as
Jacques once put it, that no longer spoke to contemporary needs. The philosophical and theological riches of the
past were to be unleashed and used to grapple with modern questions. This was a philosophy, not of the classroom, but on the roads of the world. This was a Thomism
with the strength and clarity to forge a synthesis among
the different branches and degrees of knowledge: "The
fundamental idea was to bring into play at one and the
same time, in the concrete problems and needs of our
mind, things we knew to be diverse in essence but which
we wanted to unify within us: reason and faith, philosophy
and theology, metaphysics, poetry, politics, and the great
rush of new knowledge and of new questions brought by
modern culture." (48) And the result? "Thomism all brist-
ling with its quills was thus thrown into the bath, and
it swam there with ease." (49)

Here in what Raissa called "these days of sun" in
France, it must have seemed like all the artistic and in-
tellectual world was coming to Meudon or being effected
by its light and warmth: Abbé Lallement and Dalbiez,
Prince Ghika and Massignon, Gheon and Cocteau, Reginald
Garrigou-Lagrange who became the spiritual director of
the Thomist circle and gave its annual retreats, Abbé
Lamy and Abbé Journet and young students like Yves
Congar and Olivier Lacombe, and so many more.

It was the animated discussions of these study meetings, retreats and Sunday afternoon gatherings which cre-

ated the atmosphere out of which the **Degrees of Knowledge** was born. The stimulus of the Thomist circle might account for the unusual procedure that Maritain followed in dedicating the **Degrees** to four different people. Chapter 5, Metaphysical Knowledge, was dedicated to Raissa in acknowledging not only her early metaphysical inspirations but her philosophical work with Jacques, starting with his first articles on Bergson which he later regretted had not appeared under their joint authorship. Chapter 6, Mystical Experience and Philosophy, was dedicated to Père Garrigou-Lagrange who had been a source of philosophical and theological inspiration to the Maritains, and Chapter IX, Todo y Nada, to Charles Henrion, a contemplative priest who followed Charles de Foucald's footsteps in the deserts of North Africa. (50)

If Maritain's first sabbatical produced his introduction to philosophy and represents the young Maritain writing a textbook, his second sabbatical which he took in 1929-1930 in order to write the **Degrees** represents the mature Maritain who has found his own distinctive way of philosophizing. He writes of these Meudon years:

"Finally and above all, it was understood instinctively that the whole carapace of words is absolutely nothing when the words are employed to facilitate some intuitive discovery. I must add that the experience of our study meetings taught me a very precious thing: namely, that discursive and demonstrative argumentation, doctrinal erudition and historical erudition are assuredly necessary, but of little efficacy on human intellects such as God made them, and which first ask to see. In actual fact, a few fundamental intuitions, if they have one fine day sprung up in a mind, mark it forever (they are intemporal in themselves), and they suffice, not doubtless to make a specialist in Thomist philosophy or Thomist theology, but to make a man unshakably strengthened in the love of St. Thomas and in the understanding of his wisdom. I observed this in a good number of our friends, whose example I take to be decisive." (51)

The very fact that Maritain took a sabbatical for the writing of the **Degrees** is an indication of the importance he gave to it. During these years he was caught up in an ever-growing press of activities and always lamenting his lack of time to fulfill all the demands made on him.

On occasion he would stay up all night correcting proofs to meet publishing deadlines. But the **Degrees** demanded special attention, for it was the articulation of the inner vision that he had nurtured with Raissa for so long.

In Chapter V, Maritain returns to the mystery of being that he was exploring in "Connaissance d'être". "I find it (being) everywhere, everywhere itself and everywhere varied." (52) "But nothing can be applied to it from the outside in order to differentiate it." (53) If being can embrace this or that individual, it must somehow transcend them. In being we obtain "an object of concept not only transindividual, but trans-specific, transgeneric, trans-categorical, as if in opening a blade of grass one started a bird greater than the world... it is polyvalent, it envelops an actual multiplicity; the bird we spoke of a moment ago is at the same time a flock." (54)

Maritain returns to the primordial fact, "All these things are", in a deeper way: "When I look at a man and think: 'This is a being,' or 'He exists,' I grasp a certain determinate being, finite, perishable, fleshly and spiritual, subject to time and (M. Heidegger would say) to anguish, and a certain existence similarly qualified. But the analogous object 'being,' 'existence,' thus thought by me outreaches this analogate in such a way that it will be found also, intrinsically and properly, in analogates **which differ from man by their very being and their very mode of existing.**" (55) The concept of being is "at once one and multiple". It is "implicitly and actually multiple" and "**one in a certain respect,** insofar as it does make incomplete abstraction from its analogates, and is disengaged from them without being conceivable apart from them, as attracted towards, without attaining, a pure and simple unity, which could alone be present to the mind if it were able to see in itself - and without concept - a reality which would be at once itself and all things. (Let us say the concept of being demands to be replaced by God clearly seen, to disappear in the face of the beatific vision.)" (56)

In the **Degrees of Knowledge** we see Maritain's own metaphysical insight increasing. The intuition of being is not just a knowledge of first principles, but it is a knowledge of being in which existence is coming to the forefront and Maritain is beginning to appreciate the subjec-

tive requirements for this kind of metaphysical seeing.
If Descartes thought it sufficient to spend a few hours
a year on metaphysics, and philosophers after Hume and
Kant refused "all proper intelligibility to existence" (57),
Maritian is glimpsing the absolutely primordial content
of existence and the central role it plays in the metaphysics of St. Thomas:

"There is much more in a hundred existing dollars than
in a hundred possible dollars. But still more, existence
is perfection **par excellence,** and, as it were, the seal of
every other perfection... Doubtless of itself it says only
positio extra nihil, but it is the positing extra nihil of
this or that. And to posit outside of nothingness a glance
or a rose, a man or an angel is something essentially diverse, since it is the very actuation of all the perfection
of each of these essentially diverse subjects. Existence
is itself varied and admits all the degrees of ontological
intensity according to the essences that receive it. If
anywhere it is found in the pure state, without an essence that receives it - in other words, if there exists
a being whose essence is to exist - existence must there
be identical with an absolutely infinite abyss of reality
and perfection." (58)

In every act of the intellect there is an intellectual
perception of being, and when this is disengaged for itself
"It constitutes our primordial philosophical intuition without which we can no more acquire the science of metaphysical realities than a man born blind acquires the science of colors. In this metaphysical intuition the principle
of identity: 'being is not non-being,' 'every being is what
it is,' is not known merely **in actu exercito** and as an
inescapable necessity for thought, its ontological necessity
is itself seen." (59) And when the knowledge of first principles is phrased in this fashion, it is but a step to
examine how this disengagement comes about.

This increment comes in Chapter VI, Metaphysics and
Mystical Experience: "The intellect may well receive,
after the manner of a sudden revelation, a knowledge of
that which constitutes the proper object of the third
level of abstraction. One who is very near to us one day
gave us the following testimony of such a knowledge:
'Before receiving the faith,' that person told us, 'it often
happened that by a sudden intuition I experienced the

reality of my own being, of the deepest, first principle
that placed me outside of nothingness. It was a powerful
intuition and its violence often frightened me; that intuition gave me, for the first time, knowledge of a metaphysical absolute.' Or again, at the sight of something
or other - a blade of grass, a windmill - a soul may
know in an instant that these things do not exist by
themselves, and that God exists. 'Suddenly' - and I am
citing the same witness - 'all creatures appeared to me
as symbols; they all seemed to have as their unique function to **point** to the Creator.'" (60) Jacques is, of course,
citing Raissa and these passages that we have been seeing
signal the power of Maritain's mature metaphysical
thought which will unfold during the rest of his life. At
this point, in the midst of writing the **Degrees,** he is not
ready to explore the implications of this existential way
of viewing the relationship between essence and existence
or the implications that experiences like Raissa's could
have for metaphysics. He will comment, for example,
about these kinds of experiences: "But, far from being
integral parts or necessary requisites of metaphysical
science, these kinds of metaphysical experiences or intuitions... transcend the proper sphere of metaphysics..." (61)
Maritain is still emphasizing metaphysics as a science and
the objective side of the intuition of being so metaphysic's subjective demands remain in shadow, but not for
long.

These texts of the **Degrees of Knowledge** were like
little gems that, once spoken, served as points of crystallization around which Maritain's metaphysical thought
would quickly coalesce. The **Degrees** appeared in late
summer of 1932 with a preface dated, as we saw, June
11th. Certainly, this date which was the anniversary of
the Maritains' baptism was no coincidence and it under-
scores again how much this book represents an answer
to their long search for the integration of the various
parts of their lives. Later that year Jacques went on to
give a course on metaphysics at the Institut Catholique
and the process of crystallization started by the **Degrees**
bore fruit, with his course forming the foundation of Sept
**leçons sur l'être et les premiers principes de la raison
spéculative,** (Seven lessons on being and the first
principles of speculative reason), a book of such

profundity that its English title, **A Preface to Metaphysics,** does not do it justice.

Meditating again and again on the mystery of being, Maritain's insight is getting keener: "...where the mystery aspect prevails the intellect has to penetrate more and more deeply the **same** object... Thus the intellect, as its habitus grows more intense, continues, as John of St. Thomas puts it, to assault its object, the same object, with increasing force and penetration, **vehementius et profundius.**" (62) He is now ready to tackle the relationship between essence and existence that forms the heart of the metaphysics of St. Thomas.

"Observe that being presents two aspects. One of these is the aspect of **essence** which corresponds particularly to the first operation of the mind. For we form concepts primarily in order to apprehend, though in many cases blindly, essences - which are positive capacities of existence." (63) Essences are now directly centered on existence. They are "positive capacities of existence." Thomism is not a philosophy that stops at essences, but rather it goes on to the actual existence of things. This or that exists. It is of the very nature of essences to be positive capacities of existence. Maritain goes on, in an important "Digression on Existence and Philosophy" to allow the long hidden existence face of being to come out and calls Thomism an "existential philosophy" (64) and thus becomes the forerunner of the existential movement in Thomism, as we shall see in a moment, that was to develop around World War II.

And if Thomism is to be really centered on existence then the Thomist metaphysican must be immersed in existence. "He must be keenly and profoundly aware of sensible objects. And he should be plunged into existence, steeped ever more deeply in it by a sensuous and aesthetic perception as acute as possible, and by experiencing the suffering and the struggles of real life, so that aloft in the third heaven of natural understanding he may feed upon the intelligible substance of things." (65)

Now there is no escaping from the subjective side of the intuition of being. The mystery of existence is present all around us in a leaf or a stone, but why don't we see it? What makes metaphysical insight such "a sublime and exceedingly rare mental endowment."? Being is all around us but "we have not looked it in the face. We think it something far simpler than it is." It is like the stolen letter in Edgar Allen Poe's, "The Purloined Letter" which is rendered invisible to the detectives searching for it by being placed right out in the open. "For the little word 'is,' the commonest of all words, used every moment everywhere, offers us, though concealed and well concealed, the mystery of being as such." (66) "Objects, all objects, murmur this being; they utter it to the intellect, but not to all intellects, only to those capable of hearing... Being is then seen in its distinctive properties, as transobjectively subsistent, autonomous and essentially diversified. For the intuition of being is also the intuition of its transcendental character and analogical value. It is not enough to employ the word being, to say 'being.' We must have the intuition, the intellectual perception of the inexhaustible and incomprehensible reality thus manifested as the object of this perception. It is this intuition that makes the metaphysician." (67)

But how can this last sentence be reconciled with Maritain's assertion in the **Degrees**? "But far from being integral parts or necessary requisites of metaphysical science these kinds of metaphysical experience or intuitions ... transcend the proper sphere of metaphysics..." Is Maritain talking of something different here than the metaphysical experiences of Raissa that he described before? No. For he cites them again in this chapter and comments: "These are, therefore, metaphysical intuitions which are a natural revelation to the soul, invested with the decisive, imperious and dominant character of a 'substantial word' uttered by reality... Evidently this intuition does not necessarily present this appearance of a species of mystical grace. But it is always, so to speak, a gift bestowed upon the intellect, and beyond question it is in one form or another indispensable to every metaphysician." (68)

Part of the answer to why this apparent divergence exists lies in Maritain turning for the first time to this subjective dimension of the intuition of being. If these metaphysical experiences are not seen to be essential from the point of view of metaphysics as a science, they play a vital role in the development of this or that individual metaphysician. And this turn by Maritain to the

subjective requirements of metaphysics is one of his
greatest achievements. But Maritain's shift of thought
illustrates a more subtle and difficult problem of how the
various contemplations he describes interact inside us, and
we will look at this problem later.

Maritain's intuition of being is now revealed in both
its objective and subjective dimensions. He describes it
as "a genuine intuition, a perception direct and immediate, an intuition not in the technical sense which the
ancients attached to the term, but in the sense we may
accept from modern philosophy. It is a very simple sight,
superior to any discursive reasoning or demonstration,
because it is the source of demonstration. It is a sight
whose content and implications no words of human speech
can exhaust or adequately express and in which in a
moment of decisive emotion, as it were, of spiritual
conflagration, the soul is in contact, a living, penetrating
and illuminating contact, with a reality which it touches
and which takes hold of it. Now what I want to emphasize is that it is being more than anything else which
produces such an intuition." (69) This is, of course, an
echo of **La Philosophie Bergsonienne** and Maritain is
aware that his intuition could be mistaken for Bergson's,
so he insists "he (Bergson) denies his intuition is intellectual. I, on the other hand, have just maintained that the
object par excellence of intuition is being, but that that
intuition is intellectual." (70)

But instead of discarding Bergson's genuine insights
Maritain will try to reconcile these two views of intuition, by taking Bergson's intuition and other similar approaches and seeing how they can serve as "concrete approaches which prepare for this intuition and lead up to
it." (71) He describes Marcel's fidelity, Heidegger's
anguish, a "feeling at once keen and lacerating of all
that is imperiled in our existence" and Bergson's duration.
Now when we remember that it was duration that served
as Maritain's road to the intuition of being, this description takes on personal overtones:

"Duration is apprehended by an experience of motion
in which, on a level deeper than consciousness, our psy-
chic states fuse in a potential manifold which is, notwith-
standing, a unity, and in which we are aware of advancing through time and enduring through change indivisibly,

yet we are growing richer in quality and triumphing over the inertia of matter. This is a pyschological experience which is not yet the metaphysical intuition of being, but is capable of leading us up to it. For involved in this psychological duration and implicitly given by it there is indeed existence, the irreducible value of being, **esse.**

"This intuition is therefore a path, an approach, to the perception of existence. The latter, however, is not yet nakedly displayed in its own intelligible form." (72) Even though Maritain attained a glimpse of the intuition of being through duration he is insisting on the difference between an existential Thomism and the modern existentialisms of various persuasions. There are many concrete manifestations of existence that can prepare us "to recover the sense of being. But they can do this only if we will travel further; cross the threshold, take the decisive step ... We do this by letting the veils - too heavy with matter and too opaque - of the concrete psychological or ethical fact fall away to discover in their purity the strictly metaphysical values which such experiences concealed." (73)

When we have disengaged being in its full intelligibility, being as being, what do we see? It is as it were "a pure activity, a subsistence, but a subsistence which transcends the entire order of the imaginable, a living tenacity, at once precarious - it is nothing for me to crush a fly - and indomitable - within and around me there is growth without ceasing." (74) It is the task of metaphysics as a science to explore this mystery and express it in a rigorously conceptual way, ever mindful that this expression will never exhaust the mystery of being. The intuition of being is an abstractive or eidetic intuition or visualization that produces an idea. It is the mind that through the intuition of being discovers an imperfect and relative unity in the diversity of actually existing things.

"But in virtue of its essential structure the concept of being also includes in itself indissolubly... these two linked and associated members of the pair essence-existence, which the mind cannot **isolate** in separate concepts." (75) Now we are approaching the content of the intuition of being which is closely allied to the content of philosophical or metaphysical contemplation. But before we look at this content two further points ought to be made.

First, **Sept leçons** presents Maritain at his metaphysical finest. He is not a writer of textbooks. He needs a greater freedom to spread his wings and soar and to let the lightning of his own intuition flash. Perhaps this is why he never completed a proposed series of textbooks that had been initiated with his introduction to philosophy which had been followed by a text on logic. In his preface to these seven lessons he mentions that his publisher Pierre Téqui had been receiving letters asking whether this series of textbooks would be continued. Maritain's response sheds a little more light on his methodology. No. He has not renounced the proposed series, but such a collection of textbooks must be built on more detailed studies such as **Réflexions** and **Les Degrés** and now **Sept leçons.** Then once this ground work had been prepared it could be summarized in a textbook. Maritain never did write a metaphysics textbook, but was that an irreplaceable loss? I don't think so. **Sept leçons** is alive and vibrant and conveys, better than any textbook, the message of the indispensable role of the intuition of being in the creation of metaphysics.

The second point is more important. Traditionally the period around World War II has been looked at as the time when the central role of the act of existence, or esse, in St. Thomas was rediscovered after centuries of neglect. Indeed, this rediscovery was rightly acclaimed as one of the finest achievements of the 20th century's Thomistic renaissance. But the exact chronology of these events has never been made clear. For example, the 5th edition of Etienne Gilson's Le Thomisme, which was written in 1943, is credited as one of the instigators of this development of an existential Thomism. But when we read the pages of the chapter "L'esprit du Thomisme" we see that Gilson cites two contemporary works. One is Joseph de Finance's **Etre et agir dans la philosophie de Saint Thomas** (Being and action in the philosophy of St. Thomas) which appeared in 1943, but had been in preparation for many years. This citation is readily understandable, for **Etre et agir** was de Finance's doctoral dissertation and was done under Gilson's direction, and de Finance's position did not depend on either Gilson or Maritain. He attributes the origin of his insights to his

Jesuit confreres who held to the real distinction of essence and existence, the remark of one of them that esse was an **act**, and especially his reading of St. Thomas. (76)

The other citation of Gilson's is to Maritain's **Sept leçons.** "...The proper object of the intellect is being" writes Gilson, and then quotes Maritain "not only as 'essential' or quiddative but existential" and a little later "the Thomist philosophy is an existential philosophy". (77) But even though Maritain was one of the originators of an existential Thomism it was not until 1947 and **Existence and the Existent,** dedicated again to Raissa, that he more fully explores its implications and the relationship between essence and existence.

Existence and the Existent is "an essay on the existentialism of St. Thomas Aquinas" (78) and what distinguishes an authentic Thomism "is precisely the primacy which authentic Thomism accords to existence and to the intuition of existential being." (79) This intuition has to do most of all with the relationship between essence and existence. "The most fundamental and most characteristic metaphysical thesis of Aristotelianism as re-thought by Thomas Aquinas, the thesis of the real distinction between essence and existence in all that is not God - in other words, the extension of the doctrine of potency and act to the relation between essence and existence, is directly connected with this intuition." (80) And now Maritain caps 40 years of probing the mystery of being with an ever deeper look at the relationship between essence and existence.

"...Existence is not an essence. It belongs to another order, an order which is other than the whole order of essences." (81) But "...the concept of existence cannot be detached from the concept of essence. Inseparable from each other, these two make up one and the same concept, simple although intrinsically varied; one and the same essentially analogous concept, that of being." (82) "Existence is always the existence of something, of a capacity to exist. The very notion of **essentia** signifies a relation to **esse,** which is why we have good grounds for saying that existence is the primary source of intelligibility." (83) "...The metaphysics of St. Thomas is centered, not upon essences but upon existence - upon the mysterious gushing forth of the act of existing in which, according to the analogical variety of the degrees of being, qualities and natures are actualised and formed, which qualities and natures refract and multiply the transcendent unity of subsistent Being itself in its created participations..." (84) And finally in a passage ablaze with Maritain's own intuition of being: "We can understand nothing of this... if we do not see that the very intelligibility of essences is a certain kind of ability to exist... The analogical infinity of the act of existing is a created participation in the unflawed oneness of the infinity of the **Ipsum esse subsistens;** an analogical infinitude which is diversified according to the **possibilites** of existing." (85)

This passage is a window that looks on to the heart of the metaphysics of St. Thomas, but only if we can see, if we possess that inner spiritual seeing that Maritain called the intuition of being. When he says "the very intelligibility of essences is a certain kind of ability to exist" we have to understand that essences are not somehow pre-existing receptacles which receive existence, but are simply potencies or capacities for existence. An essence is this or that particular capacity to receive a certain amount, as it were, of existence; what makes an essence to be an essence is this capacity for existence.

Maritain continued to return to contemplate the mystery of being and try to penetrate its inexhaustable depths more deeply. By December of 1965, at 83 years old, he had completed **The Peasant of the Garonne** in which he talked at length about the intuition of being in a vocabulary which is now familiar to us: The human mind is an intellect, "a power capable of **seeing** in the intelligible order as the eye **sees** in the sensible order..." (86) and he goes on to cite his **Sept leçons** and the experience of Raissa. And while critical of the then popular phenomenologies, he is well aware of the deficiencies of a scholasticism in which the intuitive fires have been covered by the routines of reason, which is exemplified by the Thomism of the manuals which is like "an aerolite which has fallen from the sky, with everything we need to know written on it." (87)

A genuine Thomistic metaphysics is very different in origin. "There is nothing simpler to think **I am, I exist,** this blade of grass exists; this gesture of the hand, this captivating smile that the next instant will hurry away, **exist**; the world **exists.** The all-important thing is for such a perception to sink deeply enough within me that my awareness of it will strike me some day sharply enough (at times violently) to stir and move my intellect up to that very world of preconscious activity, beyond any word or formula... And then, if luck should take a hand, and if the eye of the consciousness, sufficiently accustomed to the half-light, should penetrate a little, like a thief, this limbo of the preconscious, it can come about that this simple I am will seem like a revelation in the night ..." (88)

If this intuition is not the intuition of Bergson "...it is nevertheless thanks to the impact of the latter, and of Bergson's metaphysical genius, on modern thought... that contemporary Thomists have at last recognized (not without opposition, nor yet unanimously; there are not that many metaphysicians in the world) the essential and absolutely rockbottom importance of the intuition of being in their own philosophy. From this point of view one ought to consider Bergson a great liberator." (89) There is a certain serenity and balance in this passage that is the fruit of Maritain's long struggle to define his relationship with Bergson. The intuition of being is completely Thomist in content, but Bergson inspired Maritain to bring to conscious awareness and development this dimension of the philosophy of St. Thomas.

In a talk given in Kolbsheim in the summer of 1967 called "Reflexions sur la nature blessée" (Reflections on wounded nature) Maritain returns once again to the intuition of being, and remarkably at age 84, attempts to deepen his thought, this time with a nod to Heidegger. He describes several distinct concepts of being. In the first we say, "That rose is there." And this says nothing more than that this rose is present to my world. This first concept of existence is conceived in the mode of an essence and closed up in the sphere of sensible experience. It simply declares the rose present in the way common sense would do.

In contrast, the second concept of being, which is the intuition of being itself, unleashes the full intelligibility of this "is". In fact, this concept of existence is not like other concepts that precede an act of judgment and are

united in it, but it is a unique concept that comes after
the judgment of existence. "The intelligence, in the instant that the eye sees this rose, and says: that rose is
there, passes to a superior level... which is also a moment of natural contemplation... then the lightning of the
intuition of being flashes and the **to be** of the rose, in-
tentionally present already in the intelligence... as implicitly and blindly contained in 'that rose is there'... is revealed as an object now explicitly seized..." (90)

Finally, in an article that appeared in the **Revue
Thomiste** in 1970, "Pas de savoir sans intuitivité" (No
knowledge without intuition) and was collected, together
with "Reflections on wounded nature", under the heading
of "For an existential epistemology", in Maritain's last
book, **Approches sans entraves,** (Approaches without obstacles), in 1973, Maritain completed the circle begun with
his 1910 article which had started off with a discussion
of reason and intuition. Here Maritain explores the constant role of intuition in the creation of concepts, the
judgment and in the process of reasoning. The interaction
between intuition and reasoning is like an explorer who
will send out scouts of intuition and then consolidates
their findings by sending out the mapmakers of reason.
And intuition, by keeping a constant eye on the real,
prevents reason from losing sight of the path it should
follow. Finally, Maritain sums up his lifelong reflection
on the nature of intuition by saying: "There is no understanding without intuition." (91)

We have arrived much closer to our goal of understanding Maritain's metaphysical contemplation. It is going
to be a contemplation that gazes into the very ontological depths of things where the very what or essence of
things shows its deepest face, which is existence. And
this existing essence, this existent, draws us further to
the center of the mystery of being where God dwells. In
the metaphysics of Maritain, as in that of St. Thomas,
the question of God is not something added to it from
the outside out of some misplaced piety, but it emerges
at its absolute center as we pursue the most obvious of
facts, the what and that of things, to their final conclusion.

As far back as **La Philosophie Bergsonienne** Maritain
has expounded with clarity and zest the arguments of St.

Thomas for the existence of God. By the time we reach
the **Degrees of Knowledge** these Thomistic proofs, long
since assimilated, begin to take on a distinctive Maritain-
ian flavor: "A philosopher thinks and grasps reflexively
his own act of thought. Here is a reality that has a certain ontological quality or value and the existence of
which **hic et nunc** is indubitable to him... Morever, this
philosopher knows that his thought which is a mystery of
vitality to the world of bodies is at the same time a
mystery of debility in itself. For it is subject to error
and to time, to forgetfulness and to sleep, to distractions
and to apathies... And so it is clear to our philsopher
that he himself is not thought. He **is** not thought; he **has**
thought. But if he has it without being it, does he derive
it from something other than himself; from a cause?...
From the moment there are diverse things, no one suffices unto itself to exist." (92) "From the moment that
there are diverse things", from the moment we grasp essence existing, and truly grasp the relationship between
essence and existence, then "no one suffices unto itself
to exist". If every essence is a certain capactiy to exist
no one of these contractions of what existence is in itself suffices to explain existence. The very fundamental
facts that are the starting point of metaphysical inquiry
lead to the existence of God, but only if we have the
metaphysical insight, the intuition of being to see beyond
the surface of these facts. "Existence is itself varied and
admits all the degrees of ontological intensity according
to the essences that receive it." (93) But existence received demands existence unreceived. Every essence is
a positive capacity for existence, but these positive capacities could not receive existence if there were not
something that is existence unreceived by essence, existence itself.

Now we can understand more clearly the passage
where Maritain writes of the concept of being: "Let us
say that the concept of being demands to be replaced by
God clearly seen, to disappear in the face of the beatific
vision." (94) The intuition of being allows us to grasp the
mind's inner dynamism which urges it to search for the
deepest ontological core of the things around us and
within us, as well. In 1947 in an essay, "A New Approach
to God" Maritain shows how the intuition of being has

at its heart God's existence:

"Once a man... has really perceived this tremendous
fact, sometimes exhilarating, sometimes disgusting and
maddening: I **exist**, he is henceforth taken hold of by the
intuition of Being and the implications it involves... When
it takes place, I suddenly realize that a given entity,
man, mountain, or tree, exists and exercises that sovereign activity **to be** in its own way, in an independence
from **me** which is total, totally self-assertive and totally
implacable. And at the same time, I realize that I also
exist, but as thrown back into my loneliness and frailty
by such affirmation of existence in which I have positive-
ly no part... I see that Being-with-nothingness, as my own
being is, implies, in order to be, Being-without-nothing-
ness - that absolute existence which I confusedly perceived as involved in my primordial intuition of existence." (95)

The intuition of being, both as a way of seeing and
in its content, finds its supreme object in God. Neither
Maritain nor St. Thomas before him would ever say that
by this intuition we see God directly, but rather we know
him through the prism of creatures. Everything that
exists around us by the simple fact that it does exist in
this or that particular way, points to Existence itself. If
we can see clearly and deeply enough we can know that
God exists, but this is a knowledge that does not deliver
God up to us, but starting from the mirror of creatures,
rises to a knowledge of God which, while certain and
true, is swallowed up in the darkness where God dwells.
If we push our knowledge of things enough we will arrive
at a genuine knowledge of God, but because this knowledge starts from the limited things around us it is
wrapped up in a mode of signification that is limited and
cannot be directly and immediately applied to God. We
must distinguish between "what is signified" and the
"mode of our conception". (96)

What does this mean when it comes to being itself?
Our knowledge of the being of creatures leads us to say
that God is a being, but we must immediately qualify
this statement. God does not have essence and existence
like we do. His existence is not received and limited by
his essence. His essence is not a certain positive capacity
for existence; his existence is unlimited and unreceived

and is identical to his essence. We are correct in saying
that from the existence of creatures we can know that
God exists, but this does not deliver into our hands a
direct knowledge of God, but rather what Maritain calls
an uncircumscriptive knowledge in which we see that the
essence-existence structure found in creatures demands
existence in all its purity, but we do not see God in his
essence. In short, we have a very precious but limited
knowledge of God.

Further, if I am a person, someone who knows and
loves, then God must be a person as well, but in some
way too wonderful for me to grasp. And the intuition of
being "normally carries along with itself another intuition,
the intuition of my own existence or my Self, the intuition of Subjectivity as Subjectivity. Now Subjectivity,
insofar as it is Subjectivity, is not an object presented
to thought, but rather the very wellspring of thought -
a deep, unknown and living center which superabounds in
knowledge and superabounds in love, attaining only
through love its supreme level of existence, existence as
giving itself... And not only does he know, by virtue of
his primordial intellectual grasping of existence, that God
exists and is the absolute Being, the self-subsisting **Esse.**
He also knows that because of this very fact, God is
absolute ontological generosity, the self-subsisting Love;
and that such transcendent Love inherently causes,
permeates and activates every creature, which in answer
loves God more than itself." (97)

It is in understanding the inner movement that gives
birth to this kind of knowledge of God that we have finally arrived at the proximate means of understanding
metaphysical contemplation. In a postscript to his last
metaphysical essay, "No Knowledge without Intuition",
Maritain explains the nature of metaphysical contemplation. It is in metaphysics that the intuitivity of the intellect finds its highest natural exercise. And when someone
has developed this metaphysical insight especially by
directing it towards God, "metaphysics culminates in a
kind of contemplation that could be called **philosophical
contemplation** and which, as in all contemplation, com-
prises a certain superior sort of intuition." (98)

How does this philosophical contemplation come about?
"When the philosopher does not content himself with

naming such and such uncreated perfection giving it a
quick nod before passing to the next, but sets himself to
meditate on it and what he knows of divine things, he
experiences that his intelligence and all his ideas are
surpassed by them and are disproportionate to them; and
the more he fixes his spirit on the ideas that make him
know God, the more he experiences the devouring power
of this surpassing and disproportion and of the night in
which - at the instant when the signs here below, which
proceed from him, make us utter his name - God hides
from our human eyes." (99)

This kind of contemplation can be accompanied by a
natural love of God and a fear of trembling closely related to adoration. But it is a contemplation which does not
bear directly on God, "but on that which happens in the
knowing subject and on the disproportion of his concepts
in regards to the object he knows." (100) But if intuition
must somehow have a rapport with the object known,
which in this case is God, then how does it take place?
Our natural metaphysical knowledge of God is both a
knowing and an unknowing. We know that God exists and
that his essence is his existence, but we cannot see this
existence. Every created thing with the whole force of
its being points to God but as we follow these pointers
we are swallowed up in darkness.

"But what! This sting of negativity, this unknowing
which accompanies and surpassed invincibly the knowledge
in the knowing subject, is it not in this subject the re-
versed image of something infinitely positive in God, the
negative image in us of the **divine sublimity**?" This cultivated metaphysical intuition "seizes in a flash, in an in-
stantaneous perception" this negative knowledge in the
subject and "reverses it in changing its sign" so that "the
dazzled intellect plunges in it as in a luminous abyss that
overflows it in every direction." (101)

All the elements of Maritain's metaphysical development find fulfillment in this doctrine of metaphysical
contemplation: his apprenticeship with Bergson, the metaphysical experiences of Raissa, the philosophical demands
implicit in faith, the metaphysical doctrine of St.
Thomas with its primacy of existence or esse, and Maritain's own discovery of the subjective dimension of
metaphysics. This last element, while momentarily

neglected today, may well be one of his greatest achievements. A serene objectivity was the hallmark of the philosophy of St. Thomas without a word about how he personally came to his revolutionary insight on the role of esse. But Maritain, heir at once to the modern sense of subjectivity and to the metaphysics of St. Thomas, made conscious for the first time the inner personal requirements for metaphysical activity which he summed up under the heading of the intuition of being. And it is this intuition that allowed him to attain such a deep grasp of that contemplation which is the crown of metaphysics.

Maritain was always fond of diagrams so I am going to risk creating one of my own in order to illustrate what he meant by metaphysical contemplation.

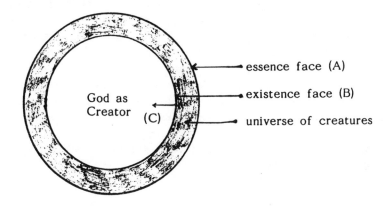

God as
Creator
(C)

essence face (A)

existence face (B)

universe of creatures

We usually experience the things around us as if we are standing at position (A). This is the essence face of the circle of created beings. From this perspective we see a bird or a tree or a stone. We focus on the differences among things. A bird is a bird and it is not a tree. We live in a world of essences (existing) but existence is bracketed and we have no yet averted to it for itself. We notice it in the form of Maritain's first concept of existence in which we say, "Here is a bird" or "There is a tree". Existence means no more than being present; we have not yet unleashed the intelligibility of existence.

With the intuition of being, we move to the inner circle of the universe of creatures (B) which is their

existence. We then see that essence is not the ultimate
principle of a thing. An essence is a certain capacity for
the act of existing. Now we see existing essences. The
previous emphasis on the diversity of things is replaced
by a sense of their unity. This bird is a being and this
tree is a being. And this being and that being, this act
of existing and that act of existing, demands Existence
itself.   "The analogical infinity of the act of existing is
a created participation in the unflawed oneness of the
Ipsum esse subsistens." (102)

Finally if we concentrate, no longer on the existence
of creatures, but the whole thrust of this existence
which points to Existence itself, then we arrive at metaphysical contemplation. We concentrate on the center
(C). The very essence-existence structure of things, existence received by essence, impels us to affirm that Existence unreceived must be at the center of the universe
of creatures. But we don't see it and know it directly.
It is a secure knowledge - for it is founded on the most
evident and basic of facts - but it is a knowledge
wrapped in darkness. But the more we cultivate this
intuition of being centered on God, the more we realize
that this darkness is not the darkness of mere negation
and emptiness, but is a darkness of a light too bright
for our minds to comprehend. Our negative knowledge
becomes a powerful symbol of the richness of God's
existence and our intellects are in awe at this dark yet
luminous abyss.

NOTES

(1) "Pas de savoir sans intuitivité" in **Approches sans entraves,** Paris, Fayard, 1973, p. 412.

(2) Raissa Maritain, **We Have Been Friends Together,** Garden City, New York, Image Books, 1961 edition, p. 34. Translated from **Les Grandes Amitiés,** New York, Editions de la Maison Française, 1942.

(3) **Ibid.** p. 40; good biographical material in Julie Kernan, **Our Friend, Jacques Maritain,** Garden City, New York, Doubleday, 1973.

(4) **Ibid.,** p. 57.

(5) For material on the school careers of the Maritains see: Stanley Jaki, "Maritain and Science" in **The New Scholasticism,** Summer, 1984.

(6) **We Have Been Friends Together,** p. 61.

(7) **Ibid.,** p. 64.

(8) **Ibid.,** p. 70.

(9) Henri Bergson, **An Introduction to Metaphysics,** authorized translation by T.E. Hulme, New York, Putman's and Sons, 1912, p. 7.

(10) **Ibid.,** p. 9.

(11) **Ibid.,** p. 74.

(12) **We Have Been Friends Together,** p. 82.

(13) **Ibid.,** p. 115-116. Emphasis in the original.

(14) Jacques Maritain, **Notebooks,** Albany, New York, Magi Books, 1984, p. 28-29. Translated from **Carnet de notes,** Paris, Desclée de Brouwer, 1965. Emphasis in the original.

(15) **Ibid.,** p. 28.

(16) **We Have Been Friends Together,** p. 116.

(17) **Ibid.,** p. 119.

(18) **Ibid.,** p. 138.

(19) **Ibid.,** p. 143.

(20) Jacques Maritain, **Bergsonian Philosophy and Thomism,** New York, Greenwood Press, 1968, p. 16-17. Translated from **La Philosophie Bergsonienne,** third edition,

Paris, Téqui, 1948.
(21) We Have Been Friends Together, p. 156.
(22) Bergsonian Philosophy and Thomism, p. 17.
(23) Ibid., p. 20.
(24) "La Science moderne et la raison", became the lead
article in Antimoderne, Jacques and Raissa Maritain,
Oeuvres Complètes, Volume II, Editions Universitaires
Fribourg Suisse.
(25) Raissa Maritian, Adventures in Grace, printed together with We Have Been Friends Together, see note 2.
(26) Ibid., p. 342.
(27) Bergsonian Philosophy and Thomism, p. 72.
(28) Ibid., p. 102.
(29) Ibid., p. 102.
(30) Ibid., p. 27 and p. 27, note 1.
(31) Ibid., p. 30.
(32) Ibid., p. 34-35.
(33) Ibid., p. 151.
(34) Ibid., p. 150, note 2.
(35) Ibid.
(36) Ibid.
(37) Ibid., p. 153.
(38) Ibid., p. 154.
(39) Adventures in Grace, p. 352.
(40) Antimoderne, Oeuvres Complètes, Volume II, p. 960.
(41) Bergsonian Philosophy and Thomism, p. 12.
(42) Oeuvres Complètes, Volume II, p. 928.
(43) O.C., Vol. II, p. 1047.
(44) Ibid., p. 1048.
(45) Ibid., p. 1051.
(46) Ibid., p. 1053.
(47) Detailed bibliographical information can be found in
the Oeuvres Complètes, and in the various bibiliographi-
cal bulletins published by the Cahiers Jacques Maritain.
(48) Notebooks, p. 135.
(49) Ibid., p. 136.
(50) The fourth dedication was to Charles Du Bos, and
a fifth in the first French edition to Père Bruno.
(51) Notebooks, p. 136-137.
(52) Jacques Maritain, Distinguish To Unite or The
Degrees of Knowledge, Newly translated from the fourth
French edition under the direction of Gerald Phelan, New
York, Charles Scribner's Sons, 1959, p. 210. The original

is **Distinguer pour unir ou les degrés du savoir,** Paris, Desclée de Brouwer, 1932.
(53) **Ibid.,** p. 211.
(54) **Ibid.,** p. 212.
(55) **Ibid.,** p. 212-213. Emphasis in the original.
(56) **Ibid.,** p. 213-214.
(57) **Ibid.,** p. 216.
(58) **Ibid.,** p. 216-217.
(59) **Ibid.,** p. 215.
(60) **Ibid.,** p. 279.
(61) **Ibid.,** p. 279.
(62) **A Preface to Metaphysics,** New York, Mentor Omega, 1962, p. 15. Translated from **Sept leçons sur l'être et les premiers principes de la raison spéculative,** Paris, Téqui, 1934.
(63) **Ibid.,** p. 26.
(64) **Ibid.,** p. 30.
(65) **Ibid.,** p. 30.
(66) **Ibid.,** p. 88.
(67) **Ibid.,** p. 49.
(68) **Ibid.,** p. 52.
(69) **Ibid.,** p. 50-51.
(70) **Ibid.,** p. 51.
(71) **Ibid.,** p. 53.
(72) **Ibid.,** p. 53-54.
(73) **Ibid.,** p. 55-56.
(74) **Ibid.,** p. 56-57.
(75) **Ibid.,** p. 68.
(76) A letter from Joseph de Finance, Oct. 1990. Charles A. Bernard suggests the influence of André Marc and his "L'idée de l'être chez Saint Thomas et dans la scholastique postérienne, **Archives de Philosophie** V, X, Paris: G. Beauchesne et ses fils, 1933.
(77) Etienne Gilson, **Le Thomisme,** Paris, J. Vrin, 1947, note to the 5th edition dated April 20, 1943, p. 505-509.
(78) **Existence and the Existent,** Garden City, New York, Image Books, 1956, p. 11. Translated from **Court traité de l'existence et de l'existant,** Paris, P. Hartmann, 1947.
(79) **Ibid.,** p. 12.
(80) **Ibid.,** p. 44-45.
(81) **Ibid.,** p. 28.
(82) **Ibid.,** p. 34.
(83) **Ibid.,** p. 43-44.
(84) **Ibid.,** p. 51.

(85) **Ibid.**, p. 45.
(86) The Peasant of the Garonne, New York, Holt, Rhine-hart and Winston, 1968, p. 110. Translated from **Le Pay-san** de la Garonne, Paris, Desclée de Brouwer, 1966.
(87) **Ibid.**, p. 137.
(88) **Ibid.**, p. 138.
(89) **Ibid.**, p. 139.
(90) Approches sans entraves, Paris, Fayard, 1973, p. 270.
(91) **Ibid.**, p. 392.
(92) The Degrees of Knowledge, p. 222-223.
(93) **Ibid.**, p. 217.
(94) **Ibid.**, p. 213-214.
(95) The Range of Reason, New York, Charles Scribner's Sons, 1952, p. 88-89. Translated from **Raison et raisons**, Paris, Egloff, 1947, but includes additional essays.
(96) **The Degrees of Knowledge**, p. 227.
(97) The Range of Reason, p. 91-92.
(98) **Approches sans entraves**, p. 411.
(99) **Ibid.**, p. 413. "Quand le philosophe ne se contente pas de nommer telle ou telle perfection incréée en lui donnant un rapide coup de chapeau avant de passer à la suivante, mais qu'il se met à méditer sur elle et sur ce qu'il sait des choses divines, il expérimente que son intelligence et toutes ses idées sont dépassées par elles et leur sont dispropotionnées; et plus il fixe son esprit sur les idées qui lui font connaître Dieu, plus il éprouve la puissance dévorante de ce dépassement et cette disproportion, et de la nuit dans laquelle, en l'instant même où les signes ici-bas qui procèdent de lui nous font proférer son nom, Dieu se dérobe à nos yeux humains."
(100) **Ibid.**, p. 414.
(101) **Ibid.**, p. 415. "Mais quoi! Cette morsure de négativité, cette nescience qui accompagne et déborde invinciblement le savoir dans le sujet connaissant n'est-elle pas en celui-ci l'image renversée de quelque chose d'infiniment positif en Dieu, l'image négative en nous de la **divine sublimité**?... Sans doute avons-nous déjà l'idée ou le concept analogique de la sublimité divine, mais l'intuitivité de l'esprit, par la réversion qu'elle opère, vient éclairer cette idée, la faire resplendir davantage, en telle sorte que l'intellect ébloui plonge en elle comme dans un abîme lumineux qui la déborde de toutes parts."
(102) **Existence and the Existent**, p. 45.

CHAPTER II

MYSTICAL CONTEMPLATION

In the previous chapter we traced the trajectory of Maritain's metaphysical thought from his first intuition of being to his final reflections on metaphysical contemplation. In this chapter we will follow a parallel path that explores his thoughts on mystical or supernatural or infused contemplation.

Our journey will look at some of the same events in the Maritains' lives, but this time from the contemplative perspective, and we start once again with Raissa's primordial metaphysical experiences, for they had mystical overtones. She writes, for example, about Plotinus, whom she had studied in the seminar with Bergson, that he expresses himself "as much in the character of a mystic as in that of a metaphysican." (1) And could this not have been the very reason that attracted her and Jacques to him, not to mention Bergson himself? And she speaks, as well, of her forest which has become a forest of symbols pointing to their creator, and such a vivid sense of God's existence could not have but awakened in her heart a desire, still hidden and unconscious, for a loving union with that God.

But it was through Leon Bloy that the Maritains gained their first conscious awareness of the inner contemplative experience of the saints. We have seen them reading his **La Femme Pauvre,** and they considered it providential that he did not speak to them in the language of apologetics and rational arguments but rather out of his inner convictions about the Catholic faith that he nurtured in poverty and suffering. "He placed before us the fact of sanctity. Simply, and because he loved them, because their experience was so near to his own - so much that he could not read them without weeping - he brought us to know the saints and mystics." (2) So

he would read to them from Angela of Foligno or Ruys-
broeck and have them read the life and visions of Anna
Catherine Emmerich, a 19th century German nun.

Around this same time one of their friends gave them
the **Catéchisme spirituel** of Father Surin to read in which
"the scattered notions regarding contemplation which we
had found in Plotinus, in Pascal and in Léon Bloy here
had their centre of fullness and efficacy." (3) Although,
clearly, this doctrine of contemplation could not have
been fully in focus before their baptism and their years
of prayer, their months with Bloy and the reading of the
mystics had given them "a burning desire for the happiness and holiness of the saints." (4)

But still this glimpse did not take away all difficulties
for it seemed to them that to accept faith was to aban-
don philosophy, and a long struggle preceded their baptism in June of 1906. Significantly, however, the next day
Raissa went off to rest carrying with her the autobiography of Teresa of Avila with its story of the central
importance of prayer and the contemplative journey.

At the end of the summer Jacques and Raissa left for
Heidelberg, and their home on Gaisbergstrasse was to
become a novitiate where they had set times of prayer,
spiritual reading and even chapter of faults. We saw
Jacques struggling here with his philosophical vocation,
but at the same time Raissa was searching for her own
interior path. If the beauty of the contemplative life
helped draw her to faith, it was understandable that she
would conceive her own practice of the faith as a life
dedicated to prayer. Joined by Vera they immersed themselves in the classic and modern masters of the spiritual
life. They read Francis de Sales and Father Faber, **La Vie
spirituelle** of the Abbesse de Sainte-Cécile, and Ignatius
Loyola. (5)

In 1907 Raissa's interior life begins to undergo a deep
change. She is taken sick and receives the anointing of
the sick in January and it brings with it a "grace of
total abandonment to God and of the joy of suffering."
(6) She writes to Jacques' sister Jeanne: "My soul overflows with joy, with peace, with hope and with love. This
has been like another baptism. My soul felt truly liberated from sin, wholly united to the will of God." (7)

By the fall of 1907 Raissa feels that she is "the guardian of a Kingdom which I do not see."(8) This is the Kingdom of God in the soul but "what is in my soul, I do not see. I am seated at the door." (9) One day in November the door begins to open. She is at Mass and she begins to be drawn inside this Kingdom. Jacques notes in his diary for November 26: "On returning from church Raissa sits down without saying anything; I question her; she answers me with difficulty the she 'cannot speak,' that I am not to be frightened... She felt like this immediately after Holy Communion, she had time to recite the Magnificat, and to think: **In manus tuas, Domine, commendo spiritum meum**; then impossible to think or to say a single prayer, to make any voluntary movement... In the morning, after having spoken a little, she had taken the Gospel and again became absorbed. She then had a very peaceful silent prayer in which she understood the absolute gratuitousness of divine mercy, and the **pardon** which God grants to us is a real **abandonment** of Himself, a **gift** of Himself to us." (10)

While we are not going to be examining in detail the evolution of Raissa's interior life, it is important to realize that everything that Jacques is going to write on the subject of mystical contemplation is organically linked to her experiences and must be read against this background.

Jacques' experience of his own conversion, as well as that of his companions, was to become another starting point for his reflection on the nature of contemplation, for it gave him an insight into faith and how contemplation is rooted in it. Even before baptism, Jacques and Raissa had looked at faith as "a higher gift of intuition" and had asked themselves "how could we adhere to dogmatic propositions which presuppose a rational inquiry, and the content of which, we were told, although superior to reason, is supremely reasonable, but to which one adheres only when motivated and illumined by faith - an adhesion of a unique kind, foreign to any form of adhesion known to us, whether philosophical, scientific, or simply of opinion." (11) In short, if the assent of faith is not brought about by reason, then just how does it happen? They were to reflect on their own conversions and those of their friends which slowly prepared them to grasp the answer to this vital question. One of the most striking and informative conversions in this regard was

that of Ernest Psichari, Jacques' boyhood friend. Psichari
had been baptized a Catholic but had not practiced his
faith. As a young man he had fallen into despair due to
his unrequited love for Jacques' sister and had attempted
suicide. In an effort to bring purpose and discipline into
his life he joined the French army and was posted to
North Africa. Jacques and Raissa kept him informed
about their own conversions and made no secret of their
prayers for his own. As early as January 1907 Jacques had
written to him: "I hope that you will come back from
those solitudes believing in God." And slowly, in the sands
of Sahara, Psichari began to come to faith. In his **Les
Voix qui crient dans le Désert** Psichari describes both his
travels through Mauretania and his inner journey to faith:
"To every argument can be opposed an argument, and
thus appears the futility of all arguments. So if there is
no desire to enlarge one's heart, if this instinct for God
does not exist, no proof can be usefully furnished, and
no argument is efficacious." (12) In a tribute to his friend
written after his death in World War I, Jacques writes:
"It is a magnificent testimony rendered to the reality and
efficacy of grace and to the supernatural essence of
faith." (13)

Maritain's ideas on faith expressed in this essay are
vital for us if we are to gain an insight into the nature
of supernatural contemplation which mirrors the structure
of the act of faith. Jacques is struck how in Psichari's
case faith is the work of "God alone." "God spoke to the
soul in the center of the soul where the mystical look
alone penetrates and the soul listens and responds." (14)
And Maritain comments more at length: "Doubtless a
preparation of prudence and a valid foundation of apologetics are necessary for the theological act of faith. But
the **formal motive** of faith does not rest upon human
argument; faith is not a scientifically or rationally
acquired conclusion on which a supernatural mode meri-
torious for salvation is superimposed 'like gold plating
over copper,' faith is **essentially** supernatural **quoad sub-
stantiam,** and it has its root principles not in the human
truth of apologetic demonstrations, but in the very revelation of the first Truth which is, at the same time, **that
which** we believe and **that by which** we believe, just as
light is at the same time that which is seen and that by

which one sees; and this faith rests formally on a supernatural illumination and inspiration, on a grace infused
from on high which causes us to receive within us the
testimony of God." (15) Here Maritain cites St. Thomas
at length on how we believe because of the first Truth
itself, and part of Maritain's citation of St. Thomas
comes from question 14 of his **De Veritate** which is a
cryptic hint to Maritain's distinctive way of proceeding.
These theological reflections on the act of faith are no
mere speculations on the part of Maritain that he has
rescued from the past out of some antiquarian interest,
but they are once again formulations of St. Thomas that
Maritain has discovered in all their freshness because of
conversions like Psichari's and his own.

Jacques had fought a long fight before his baptism in
1906 and we should not imagine that baptism freed him
once and for all from all doubts. After the novitiate of
Heidelberg and the graces of conversion that carried him
along he once again had to struggle: "Perhaps in 1911 or
was it in 1912, I was suddenly assailed by violent temptations against the faith. Till then the graces of baptism
had been such that what I believed I seemed **to see,** it
was certainty itself. Now it was necessary for me to
learn what the night of faith is. No longer carried in
arms, I was brutally dropped to the ground. I remember
long hours of interior torture, rue de l'Orangerie, alone
in the room on the fourth floor which I had made a kind
of retreat for work. I took care not to speak of it. I
emerged from this trial, by the grace of God, very
strengthened; but I had lost my childhood. I consoled
myself by thinking that this had doubtless been necessary,
if I was to be of some service to others." (16)

It was during this time that Psichari was making his
own way to faith, and this meaningful coincidence is
something that Jacques would not have overlooked. Further, his reference to St. Thomas' **De Veritate** when
commenting on Psichari's conversion may be a reflection
of his own struggles to understand the assent of faith
better. At the Jacques Maritain Center at the University
of Notre Dame is Maritain's own annotated copy of **De
Veritate.** This is the Marietti edition of 1914, so it is
conceivable that it is the text that aided his reflections
on his own difficulties and path that Psichari followed

which had ended in his conversion with the help of
Humbert Clérissac in Febuary of 1913. These pages show
an intensive reading of question 14, **De Fide,** with phrases
like the following underlined: "faith assents to the first
truth because of itself (primae veritati propter seipsam
assentit) (Art. I, 6); and a passage on the assent of faith
engages Maritain's special attention: "Non enim assensus
ex cogitatione causatur, sed ex voluntate... Sed quia
intellectus non hoc modo terminatur ad unum ut ad pro-
prium terminum perducatur, qui est visio alicujus intelligi-
bilis; inde est quod ejus motus nondum est quietatus, sed
adhuc habet cogitationem et inquisitionem de his quae
credit, quamvis firmissime assentiat..." (For assent is not
caused by thinking but by the will... But since the intellect in this way does not arrive at one thing as being
brought to its proper term which is the vision of some
intelligible object; therefore its motion is not yet at rest
but still has thought and seeking about the things that
it believes, no matter how firmly it assents to them.)
(Art. I, 9)

It is the role of the will in the act of faith that is
going to be an important clue when Maritain tries to
understand the nature of mystical contemplation. It is
around 1912, as well, that the Maritains are discussing
contemplation with Charles Henrion who will appear later
in our story, and all three of them are questioning Fr.
Garrigou-Lagrange on contemplative matters. (17)

If the Maritains were struggling to understand the
nature of faith, they were also hard pressed to see how
to live out a contemplative vocation. During the years
that followed Raissa's first experiences of the contemplative life in Heidelberg, she continued to be inclined
toward these ways of interior prayer. When they returned
to Paris in May 1908, they soon sought spiritual direction
from Fr. Clérissac. This led them to the great gift of
St. Thomas, but it also was the occasion of serious difficulties in Raissa's life of prayer. Jacques writes in his
notebook for Dec. 11, 1909: "Visit of Father Clérissac
after lunch. Long talk afterwards with Raissa. She regrets
not having a good old Father who would guide her in
understanding her heart." Another more telling entry
appears on September 17, 1910: "Raissa tells Father Clérissac that when her half-hour of prayer is finished, she

cannot apply herself to anything, is for some time unable
to read or to speak; once or twice this state continued
the whole day. Father replies that it is absolutely necessary to reject this interior absorption and to struggle
against it (except during the time reserved for prayer),
and as soon as this time is finished to adapt oneself to
one's ordinary occupations." (18) Jacques later comments:
"Example of a certain lack of comprehension from which
Raissa suffered a great deal. In his adversion for the
'reflex spirit' Father Clérissac precipitated matters, and
did not recognize authentic demands of her spiritual life."

In 1913, as part of his systematic confrontation of
Bergson with St. Thomas, Jacques wrote an essay entitled
"L'intuition. Au sens de connaissance instinctive ou
d'inclination" (Intuition. In the sense of instinctive knowledge or by inclination) which appeared in the **Revue de
Philosophie** and the next year in his **La Philosophie Bergsonienne.** Here intuition is no longer the intuition that
is properly philosophical but takes another sense: "to
divine, to know without reasoning, to form a just idea
or correct judgment without any discursive preparation."
(19)

Once again Maritain is moved by the use that contemporary philosophy makes of "this divination-intuition" to
rediscover what to his mind is a deeper and more correct
view in St. Thomas. He insists that this knowledge is not
something apart from the intellect but "a spontaneous
exercise of the **intelligence.**" (20) The intellect ought not
to be conceived apart from the other faculties of the
soul. This knowledge by inclination in the wide sense is
above all intellectual, but it is the intellect working in
a wholistic sense through the senses and the imagination,
and through the cogitative faculty, which is a kind of
sense instinct. These faculties can create "a certain
sympathy or **connaturality...** in virtue of which the intellect will be spontaneously inclined toward this or that
judgment." (21) In addition the will can interact with the
intellect in an analogous fashion: "...as soon as there is
love the imprint of what is loved is in some way in the
will of the one who loves, not as image or likeness, but
as impetus or impulsion... And... if love is habitual that
which is loved will be constantly in him who loves, in the
manner of an impetus or an impulsion which will cease-

lessly urge him on. Then, at the least relaxation, on the slightest propitious occasion, the soul will be invaded by the thought of what is loved; and where reason could not have recognized it, love will do so... it is a question of **recognizing** and not of knowing, truth surges up in intelligence under the stimulus of love, and thus it can be said that the mind is taught by the heart." (22)

Here we reach one of the proximate foundations of Maritain's understanding of mystical contemplation. He will return again and again to the theme of connaturality and become the leading spokesperson for it in the 20th century Thomisitic renaissance. Love plays an essential role in contemplative knowledge and Maritain goes on to cite the classic passage of pseudo-Dionysius: "Hierotheus was instructed in divine things, less for having learned them than for having lived them or suffered them (non solum discens, sed patiens divina)." (23) And he concludes: "Thus it is that the seventh gift of the Holy Spirit, the gift of Wisdom, makes us judge in an experimental way of divine things and conveys their savour to us, - sapida sapientia - thereby crowning the **habitus** of charity which introduces the soul into divine familiarity, gives it a genuine congeniality, a connaturality, compassio sive connaturalitas, with the things of God..." (24) Maritain, driven by his own spiritual thirst and those of the people around him, is making the mystical tradition of the Church his own and penetrating it in a living way always in tension with contemporary spiritual problems.

In November of 1914, Humbert Clérissac died and a year later the Maritains met the man who was to become their new director, Père Dehau, whose advice to Raissa immediately put her at ease: "When you feel an interior call to recollection, never resist. Let yourself be led at the very instant. And remain with God as long as it pleases Him, without yourself interrupting (unless you are obliged to do so by a duty of charity or some other necessity)." (25) Raissa's life of prayer around this time became increasingly devoted to what she calls silent prayer or oraison which began with a period of quiet absorption or recueillement. Much later Jacques commented more precisely on the meaning to be given to these terms. Oraison as Raissa used it meant "not meditation in which the soul is occupied in considering ideas, concepts and images, but a wordless, intuitive and quite simple prayer, a loving attention to God in which the soul is primarily occupied in letting God have its way with it, and in which, as St. Thomas expresses it, it suffers divine things, in a silence void of words, concepts and images." And recueillement meant "an inner state which far from being 'concentration' due to voluntary effort, is rather a gift received, a quiet absorption of the soul which, far from being enertia, is a secret and unifying activity too deep to be perceived." (26)

Now Raissa's life of prayer goes forward more quickly. She notes in her journal for June 27, 1916: "Between 9 and 12, almost uninterrupted **oraison...** obliged to absorb myself, my mind arrested on the Person of the Father... Suddenly, keen sense of his nearness, of his tenderness, of his incomprehensible love..." (27)

In the spring of 1921 the Maritains consulted with Garrigou-Lagrange about the creation of a Thomistic study circle. The following year found them composing its guidelines in the form of a directory which later became **De la vie d'oraison.** It was accompanied by the statutes of the Thomist circle under the motto O Sapientia which recommended the study of St. Thomas and his commentators and a private vow of prayer. **De la vie d'oraison,** translated into English as **Prayer and Intelligence** gave guidance for this life of prayer and allows us to see Jacques' views on contemplation. "Christian contemplation is the fruit of the gift of Wisdom; and this gift although a **habitus** of the intelligence... depends essentially on charity, and consequently on sanctifying grace, and causes us to know God by a sort of connaturality - in an affective, experimental and obscure manner, because superior to every concept and image." (28)

Then he cites his favorite commentator on mystical matters, John of St. Thomas: "It is in virtue of the gift which God makes of himself and of the experimental union of love that mystical wisdom attains the knowledge of divine things, which are united more closely to us, more immediately felt and tasted by us by means of love, and make us perceive that what is thus felt in the affection is higher and more excellent than all considerations based on the knowing faculties alone." (29)

Among the appendices to this little book are to be

found Note II on the three signs that John of the Cross
gives for discerning the time when to pass from meditation to contemplation and a significantly important note
IV, **Sur l'appel a la vie mystique et a la contemplation**
(On the call to the mystical life and to contemplation).
This note had first appeared in the form of a letter
received by the **Vie spirituelle** on January 23, 1923 and
then printed in their March issue, and should be situated
as part of the on-going discussions between Maritain and
Garrigou-Lagrange, who comments on Maritain's initiative
in the same issue, and in the wider context of the impas-
sioned debates taking place at this time about the normalcy of the call to infused contemplation and the question of acquired contemplation. More than **De la vie
d'oraison** as a whole, it gives us a sense of the maturing
of Maritain's contemplative thought. He has mastered the
basic elements of the tradition and now is venturing onto
new ground. The article addresses the much debated
thesis of Garrigou-Lagrange according to which all Christians are called to mystical contemplation as a normal
culmination of the development of the virtues and the
gifts of the Holy Spirit. Maritain wants to avoid two
misconceptions: "that the perfection of charity... is reserved to those souls alone who enjoy infused contemplation in its typical and normal form and that if a soul
does not arrive at that which one could thus call **manifest** contemplation (in its forms luminous or obscure) it
is always by its own fault." (30) His contribution to clari-
fying this question is to make some careful distinctions.
First, there are those souls that have not entered into
the mystical order and who are still under the regime of
the virtues; they experience a kind of contemplation, but
it is the "term of a discursive activity and the natural
activity of the faculties - comparable to the 'contemplation of the philosophers.'" This is similar to the contemplation we examined in Chapter I. But here in the context of faith and prayer it is a contemplation connected
to the theological virtues, as well, and ordered to the
affective activity of the will. In regards to mystical
contemplation, such a contemplation is only a "distant
predisposition".

But if someone has entered into the mystical way,
which for Maritain means that they have entered under

the habitual rule of the gifts of the Holy Spirit, there
is still an important point to be raised. These mystics
might be under the influence of either the active or the
passive gifts of the Holy Spirit. If it is a question of the
active gifts allied to an active temperament and vocation, they could still experience contemplation, not in its
classical form, but in one in which the gift of wisdom
only finds a "tempered exercise (un exercice attempéré)."
(31) The recollection that these people experienced for-
merly as the end of a discursive process would reflect
the action of the gifts and "a certain participation" of
mystical contemplation and be like a proximate disposition
to this contemplation. Further, if this kind of recollection
were now aided by the gifts of wisdom and knowledge
in a more manifest way, it would become an anticipation
or "inchoation" of the properly mystical prayer of quietude "without being quietude itself where the initiative
comes from the Holy Spirit." (32) This would be the
"ultimate disposition" to infused contemplation.

So Maritain, while affirming Garrigou-Lagrange's
thesis, nuances it and sees the possibility of people receiving contemplation in a masked form under the regime
of the active gifts of the Holy Spirit. He also comes to
the conclusion that while contemplation is theoretically
the normal goal of the spiritual life, due to circumstances beyond the control of the individual, like temperament, he or she might not arrive at contemplation without it necessarily being their own fault. If this article
begins to show Maritain as a master of mystical theology, it does so by taking the objective principles govern-
ing the study of contemplation and beginning to relate
them to vital subjective considerations. This process will
become stronger as Maritain's contemplative thought
develops.

Along with Garrigou-Lagrange, Charles Henrion was
an important influence on Maritain's thinking in this area.
Henrion, a man of deeply contemplative inclinations, had
known the Maritains from before the War and eventually
through the urging of his friends had become a priest and
gone to live in the deserts of North Africa. Unfortunately, his correspondence with the Maritains was apparently
destroyed at his request and all that remains is one
letter from Raissa to him. It is dated August 29-31, 1922

and was occasioned by Raissa sending him **De la vie d'oraison** and deals with the issue of the clarity or obscurity of mystical prayer, and it is much more like a short treatise than a normal letter, which might account for its preservation. In the realm of the mystical Raissa distinguishes an ontological level from a psychological one:

"Ontologically, the essence of mystical contemplation is, it seems to me, that it is produced **in virtue of union** and thus in a **passive** fashion, by a special will of God which leads him to give us, in some manner, knowledge of his love for us.

"Psychologically, the essence of mystical contemplation appears to me to be an experimental knowledge of God, 'God ineffably perceived.'" (33)

She continues a little later: "...in the mystical life God acts by a very special infusion of his grace which leads him sometimes to enlighten our mind, sometimes to kindle our will, sometimes to strengthen our heart, or to give us simultaneously supernatural light, ardour and strength, or to let us be aware only of the destruction of our human mode of acting, or our impotence, our nothingness." (34)

Ontologically it is the Holy Spirit who acts on the soul through his gifts. Psychologically "this passivity manifests itself above all by ligature, powerlessness, annihilation, because our faculties of knowing are utterly disproportionate to the object of contemplation which is God in Himself." (35) Contemplation, even as it deepens, maintains this note of obscurity. God "is perceived as someone who touches us and not as someone who is seen." (36)

1923 also saw Jacques publishing a study on Pascal as an apologist for the faith, who he felt had "affirmed magnificently the **supernaturality of the faith.**" (37) It is this perspective, Maritain feels, that provides the key to understanding Pascal's **Pensées**. In a more extensive work of the same year, Maritain turned to the thought of Maurice Blondel, and both of these articles were to be taken up in his **Réflexions sur l'intelligence.** Blondel had started a new trend in Catholic philosophy and theology with the publication of his **L'Action** in 1897. But what interests us here is not so much Maritain's evaluation of

Blondel but the occasion it gives him to develop his ideas
on knowledge by inclination or connaturality. While Maritain admits that the intellect by its very nature has a
certain affinity or connaturality for its object, this inclination is "purely and exclusively intellectual" (38) and
ought to be carefully distinguished from affective connaturality which "is not required of itself by the natural
activity of the intelligence." (39) Affective connaturality
finds its proper domain in the realm of practical knowledge which deals with acts to be done in contrast to
speculative knowledge which aims at things to be known.

When it is a question of a connnatural knowledge of
God, Maritain insists that natural knowledge of God cannot be confused with supernatural contemplation: "The
natural love of **God, known in his reflections,** by the
natural knowledge of analogy... is radically incapable of
connaturalizing the soul to God, of making it attain God
as living in His temple in the most intimate part of
itself and giving Himself to it in order that it would
enjoy him... and thus provoke a natural mystical contemplation of God, a natural knowledge of God by connaturality... A **natural mystical contemplation** is a contradic-
tion in terms." (40) A little later, he cites the same
passage of John of St. Thomas' **Cursus Theologicus** that
appeared in **De la vie d'oraison.**

The Maritains' intensive examination of the western
Catholic contemplative tradition continued in 1925 with
Raissa editing a collection of texts of Teresa of Avila
for the **Vie Spirituelle** under the heading, "Is it of great
usefulness for us to know the graces with which we have
been favored?" And the next year excerpts of her translation of John of St. Thomas' treatise on the gifts of the
Holy Spirit, which we have seen the Maritains so attached
to, began to appear in the same revue. Later the translation appeared in book form with a preface by Garrigou-
Lagrange, and it is worth sampling again the flavor of
their favorite mystical commentator:

"...it must be noted that love can be considered in
two ways: a) First, as it applies itself and other powers
to action. This love is restricted to the executive or effi-
cient order. It applies the agent to act. b) Secondly, as
it applies and unites the object to itself, assimilating it
through fruition and making itself thereby connatural and

proportionate to the object. Love experiences its object
with a sort of loving taste, according to the Psalmist,
Taste and see... For this reason, the intellect is carried
toward the object as something experienced, brought into
agreement with it, as it were. In this sense, love is not
considered precisely as moving, rather it belongs in the
genus of objective cause, since through experience the
object is diversely proportioned and made suitable to the
intellect." (41)

The years 1926-1932 were the time of preparation for
The Degrees of Knowledge. Toward the end of 1926,
Jacques' "Mystical Experience and Philosophy" appeared
in the **Revue de Philosophie,** as we saw in the last chapter, and various articles on John of the Cross were to
come out in the years just prior to the publication of the
Degrees. It is in this book that Maritain's thought on
mystical contemplation, which we have been seeing in
bits and pieces, as it were, finds a full and well developed exposition, but not a purely theoretical one, as
several events show.

In 1925, Charles Henrion had published a summary of
the mystical doctrine of John of the Cross and in 1929
the discalced Carmelite, Bruno de Jésus-Marie came out
with a life of John of the Cross to which Maritain added
a preface, and both these events touched him personally.
Fr. Bruno had been part of the Thomist circle before he
entered the Carmelites, and Henrion's summary of St.
John spoke to Jacques not only for its content and his
friendship with the author, but because of the providential use he saw the book serve. He recounts in his preface to Fr. Bruno's book: "I knew a youth of twenty,
haunted by the desire of deliverance, knowing not how
to attain it, who, urged on by a poetry that was false
and of the devil, had gone far in spiritual experiences
wherein the soul, emptied and overwhelmed, but not by
God, enjoyed a deceptive taste of infinite liberty and
domination, an ecstasy of nothingness. A certain person,
forseeing that, as the youth had reached the dark night
of the depths, he could only be healed by a vision of the
veritable, superhuman night, gave him an abstract of the
doctrine of St. John of the Cross, consisting of the most
significant passages of the saint's works. A fortnight later
the boy was suddenly struck down with illness; called to

his bedside, I saw him, once again, disfigured and dying;
in a few hours his death agony was to begin. He had sent
that morning for a priest, and questioned him about religion, for he was anxious to obtain further dogmatic
teaching; he had then made his confession and received
Holy Communion. 'What joy!' he said to me, 'I now know
what joy means. And it has all come about through St.
John of the Cross.' Henceforward, for me, the thought
of the saint and his doctrine will be inseparable from the
image of that predestined soul." (42)

Once again this story recalls for us how Maritain's
understanding of mystical contemplation and John of the
Cross is not mere academic interest, but is intertwined
with his own spiritual life and those of the people around
him. For the same reason he could have little sympathy
for a work as genuinely erudite as Jean Baruzi's **Saint
Jean de la Croix et le problème de l'experiénce mystique**
about which he writes: "Despite my friendship for you,
my dear Baruzi, I must confess that in turning a Leib-
nizian light on John of the Cross, you have erred. In
wrenching his contemplation from that which was the life
of his life (infused grace and the working of God within
him), in making him some sort of giant of the metaphysics to come... you have traced out a picture of the saint
which the latter would have held in abomination... This
theopath does not suffer things Divine, but a disease of
the Sorbonne." (43)

Part II of **The Degrees of Knowledge,** entitled "The
Degrees of Suprarational Knowledge", starts with Chapter
VI, "Mystical Experience and Philosophy" dedicated to
Garrigou-Lagrange. In this chapter Maritain is aiming at
answering the question: "Is there an authentic mystical
experience in the natural order?" And by way of providing
us the context for his answer he gives us a brilliant but
very condensed summary of the nature of mystical experience which helps us situate the Maritains' previous
remarks on this subject. Mystical experience is an **"experimental knowledge of the deep things of God."** To understand this knowledge we must distinguish natural knowledge of God in which he is known in the mirror of
creatures - which we looked at in Chapter I and in the
citation of Maritain's work on Blondel - from supernatural knowledge of God which knows God as He is in His

own life, "in His inwardness." (44)

This supernatural knowledge can be divided further
into a knowledge which is the vision we have of God in
heaven and which "knows Him by and in His very
essence" (45), and a knowledge by faith which knows the
same object, i.e., God in His inwardness, but "without
seeing it." (46) This knowledge by faith takes three distinct forms. In the act of faith God is known as He has
formally revealed Himself. In theology, reason enlightened
by faith draws out the implications of what has been
formally revealed. Finally, there is the knowledge which
is mystical contemplation in which we experience what
is known in faith, and this is the knowledge that Maritain
wants to deal with. This kind of knowledge, he insists,
is not any sort of vision of God, but is rooted in faith.
The act of faith "attains God's inner depths, His very
selfhood... without seeing it" (47), and knows God by
means of formally revealed concepts. This disproportion
between the object known and the means by which it is
grasped is the reason why faith places in the soul "at
least radically, an unconditional desire for mystical contemplation..." (48)

Mystical experience always remains rooted in faith and
an understanding of this supernatural contemplation requires that we look at the indwelling of God in our souls
and the special kind of connatural knowledge that comes
through charity. The indwelling of the divine persons
means that we live the very life of God by participation.
But how is this possible? "How can a finite subject formally participate in the nature of the Infinite?" The soul
is infinite by its relationship with the object which is God
Himself, in His inwardness, known and loved. If this
indwelling and union could be called the basic ontological
foundation of mystical contemplation, then its proximate
foundations are to be found in the gifts of the Holy
Spirit and knowledge by connaturality. The gifts are dis-
positions that "make the soul **thoroughly mobile** under
divine inspiration." (49) They are "sails set to receive the
wind of heaven." (50)

It is by charity we share in God's nature and become
connatured to him. Charity "loves Him in Himself and by
Himself." (51) And here Maritain returns to citing John
of St. Thomas in a passage where the commentator pro-

claims that love becomes the very medium by which we know God in an experimental way, as touched and tasted: "...even though faith rules love... yet in virtue of this union in which love clings to God immediately, the intellect is, through a certain affective experience, so elevated as to judge divine things in a way higher than the darkness of faith would permit." (52) While this mystical knowledge is not immediate in the sense of a vision or intuition of God, and it knows the same object that faith proposes, it knows this object in a higher mode than through images drawn from creatures. God is known through his effects "that is by the very effects that he produces in the affections and at the very root of the powers, effects which are like a taste or touch whereby he is spiritually experienced in the darkness of faith." (53)

Maritain has structured these preliminary remarks in such a way that they lead to the answer of the question that he has proposed for himself. "Is there an authentic mystical experience in the natural order?" His answer is an emphatic no. Anything else, he feels, would compromise the distinction between nature and grace which is at stake when we speak of an experience of God's inner depths in contrast to God's presence in all things in virtue of His creation of them. Even our intellect, which strives to know all things, cannot know God in His inwardness by its own power because it is not proportionate to such a lofty object, and the natural love we have of God cannot create the kind of connaturality that would give birth to the kind of knowledge that comes from infused contemplation. It cannot give us a "felt contact with God." (54)

But what of the mystical experiences found in the non-Christian religions? Don't they demonstrate the existence of a natural mystical experience? This is a question that will occupy us in detail in Chapter III, but even in this case Maritain, while admitting the probability of genuine mystical experience among non-Christians, will assert that it comes through grace and is not a "natural experience of the depths of God." (55)

Having dealt with this central issue, he asks: "Does metaphysics of itself demand mystical experience?" (56) And again the answer is no. It is in this context that he

touches on the issue of metaphysical experiences that
give rise to metaphysics as a science that I commented
on in Chapter I. There we saw that since he is looking
at the objective requirements of metaphysics and not its
subjective demands, and because he is in the midst of
talking about mystical experience as an objective completion of metaphysics, he answers that neither metaphysical
experiences like Raissa's nor mystical experiences are
necessary to metaphysics in itself. But this is not all that
Maritain has to say about the matter. If metaphysics and
mysticism are distinct in themselves, there is still "a
**factual dependence within the subject and by reason of
the subject** of metaphysics in respect to mystical experience." (57) This means that in this or that particular
individual lights of a higher order coming from faith and
mystical experience can strengthen metaphysical insight.
Without metaphysics being dependent in itself on these
other lights they can concretely aid the metaphysican to
see more clearly.

Chapter VIII of the **Degrees** is called "St. John of the
Cross; Practitioner of Contemplation", and it is Maritain's
attempt to apply to St. John's doctrine what he calls the
"fundamental thesis of this book: there are in the world
of the mind structural differentiations and a diversity of
dimensions whose recognition is of the greatest importance. Serious misunderstandings can be avoided only by
assigning to each type of thought its exact situation in
this sort of transcendental topography." (58) The issue at
stake is just where in this transcendental topography the
works of St. John should be located. Maritain's answer
has given rise to some misunderstandings, for he will call
St. John's work a practical science of contemplation, and
some people have seen this as implying that John of the
Cross was really not a genuine theologian like St. Thomas
and that his writings are being relegated to the domain
of pious literature. If Maritain were doing this, he would
be perpetuating the very split between theology and spirituality that we are looking to him to heal, and in fact
such a position is the farthest thing from his mind. What
he is doing is simply carrying out his overall plan and
asking how we can best understand St. John by seeing
where he fits on the map of the various degrees of
knowledge. The very use that he and Raissa made of St.

John's writings is enough to indicate the esteem they had for him. Further, Maritain is writing his most detailed analyses of St. John after 1926 when the Spanish mystic had been declared a doctor of the Church.

What, then, does Maritain mean by a practical science of contemplation? He reasons that St. John's primary intent in his commentaries is "to know, no longer for the sake of knowing, but for the sake of acting." (59) He is not interested in telling us what holiness is, but in leading us to it, and this goal shapes the very structure and texture of his writings. In St. Thomas we can find a speculatively practical science of contemplation, "a sure and certain speculative elucidation of mystical theology" (60), but St. John creates what Maritain calls a practically practical science which follows a different style of conceptualizing, for "the question here is to prepare for action and to assign its proximate rules." (61)

Once we grasp this fundamental distinction it gives us a powerful tool with which to understand St. John's writings. Maritain finds a fundamental agreement between St. John and St. Thomas which he demonstates by two examples. The first is the final end of human life, which both find in our transformation in God through love. The second deals with the nature of faith which, as we have seen, always fascinated Maritain. For him St. John's lines starting: "O crystalline fount. If on thy silvered surface Thou wouldst of a sudden form the eyes desired which I bear outlined in my inmost parts!" in the **Spiritual Canticle** and the saint's commentary on it, proclaim a doctrine like St. Thomas'. Faith is the fount, the silvered surface, the articles of faith and the "eyes desired" are "the very substance of faith itself." (62) Maritain finds fundamentally the same doctrine in St. Thomas, especially in the **Summa Theologiae** II,II,1,2,c, where St. Thomas declares that faith terminates not in propositions but in God, and concepts make it proportionate to us. Thus there is a certain disproportion between the object of faith, which is God in His inwardness, and our grasp of this object through God-given yet still limited human concepts, a disproportion that caught Maritain's attention in **De Veritate** as well, as we saw.

It is in the midst of this disproportion that Maritain situates mystical experience which attains the same object that faith proposes so that it is always a contemplation in faith, but attains this object in a non-conceptual, supernatural mode. And it does this by love "which inviscerates us within things divine and itself becomes the light of knowledge, in that purely and ineffable spiritual awareness given by the Holy Spirit acting through His gifts." (63)

If we fail to read John of the Cross in the practical register in which he wrote, we will misinterpret him. Maritain puts it more technically. We cannot confuse concepts fashioned by speculative or speculatively practical science with concepts fashioned by a practically practical science, even if they bear the same names. This does not mean that Maritain thinks any less of St. John's insights or fails to find formulas in his writings "big with speculative values" (64), but rather we must take the right epistemological perspective if we are to understand what St. John is actually saying. For example, if St. John calls contemplation a non-activity, is he contradicting St. Thomas who firmly says it is the highest activity? Not at all, for in St. Thomas' case he is looking at the matter ontologically, while St. John is taking a practical and psychological perspective. Again, when St. John talks of the substance of the soul in which God acts in contrast to the soul's faculties, is he violating the Thomistic thesis that contemplation takes place by means of the intellect and will? Or when St. John speaks of pure faith, is he opposing it to charity and the gifts of the Holy Spirit? In both cases, when we find the just perspective in which to read the Carmelite saint, the difficulties disappear.

One of the places where the need for this kind of understanding is most urgent is St. John's language about the complete renunciation necessary in order to arrive at divine union, his nothing, nothing, nothing. As Maritain graphically puts it, St. John is not advocating "the slightest ontological destruction of the least vein in the wing of the smallest gnat." Rather, he is speaking of an inner moral self-surrender and a giving up of the natural working of the faculties when God is calling the soul in a proximate way to contemplation.

All these things show how intensive is Maritain's reading of John of the Cross and how much he found him in

harmony with his master St. Thomas when it is a question
of the "experimental knowledge of love and union" which
is contemplation. (65) In fact, St. John cites St. Thomas
on contemplation, and Maritain summarizes this area
where the teaching of the two doctors formally inter-
sected: "charity, as it increases, transforms us in God,
whom it attains immediately in Himself, and since this
increasingly perfect spiritualization cannot be achieved
without its repercussions in knowledge, because spirit is
interior to itself, the Holy Spirit uses this very loving
transformation in God, this supernatural connaturality, as
the proper means to delectable and penetrating knowledge
which, in turn, renders the love of charity as possessive
and fruitful as is possible here below." (66)

This teaching of St. Thomas is the teaching of St.
John although, as Maritain insists, it is framed in concepts of a different texture. For St. John contemplation
is "not only for love it is **by** love: 'God never grants
mystical wisdom without love, since love itself infuses
it.'" (67) Maritain continues the citation of St. John at
great length and his whole exposition in the **Degrees** is
one of the most profound commentaries on the doctrine
of the mystical doctor.

Maritain, with his distinguish in order to unite, resists
the perennial temptation to solve a problem by allowing
one kind of knowledge to devour other kinds, even when
it is in the realm of wisdom. There is a variety of
wisdoms. "If to know is what you want - and knowledge
must be desired - study metaphysics, study theology. If
divine union is what you want, and you succeed in attaining it, you will know a great deal more, but precisely in
the measure that you go beyond knowledge... Beyond
knowing? That is to say, in love; in love transilluminated
by the Spirit, compenetrated by intelligence and wisdom."
(68) And to bring this Chapter VIII to a close Maritain
returns to an earlier theme: "...to ask metaphysics to lead
to the highest contemplation would, therefore, only
betoken a vast ignorance both of metaphysics and contemplation; to consider reason as inefficacious, of itself,
in metaphysics unless it be vivified by a knowledge by
mystical connaturality, is no less an offense against the
essential order of things." (69)

Chapter IX is dedicated to Charles Henrion, and is

entitled, following John of the Cross, **Todo y Nada,** All
and Nothing. St. John likens the soul experiencing divine
union to a window transformed in the light of the sun,
for the soul becomes God by participation: "God com-
municates to it His supernatural Being, in such wise that
it appears to be God Himself..." (70) and Maritain insists
that "Contemplation is the very experience of union." (71)
But how can we ask this sublime union of the "most
complex and weakest of creatures?" It is here that we
encounter St. John's nights. These nights are not the
nights that philosophy knows. These nights go much
deeper and "such conduct would be insane were it not
instigated by God." (72) These nights penetrate so deeply
because the goal is so lofty, an actual transformation in
God, and since this transformation takes place by love
the soul must not cling to any creature or to the natural
workings of the faculties of sense or imagination, intellect, memory or will, for none of these limited ways of
proceeding have the capacity of reaching divine union.

Maritain comments: "I realize how rash it is to summarize in a few lines a teaching of such incomparable
plenitude, transcending all philosophy, and so run the risk
of falsifying." (73) And it would be even rasher for us
to try to summarize Maritain's summary of St. John,
especially in this chapter that will culminate with a discussion of the highest level of mystical experience.
Suffice it to say that the dark night is brought about,
not principally by human effort, but by infused contemplation itself, and when the purification which St. John
calls the dark night of the soul has done its work it
leads to what the mystics call a spiritual betrothal in
which "contemplation becomes luminous" (74) and which,
in its turn, is a prelude to the highest state of mystical
contemplation, which is given the name of spiritual
marriage.

Even in this sublime state there is no identity of
being but rather one of love: "This is the order of love
as love, considered not in its ontological constituents
of essence and existence (for there it is considered as
being) but in the absolutely proper reality of the immaterial intussusception by which the other within me
becomes more me than myself." And with great delicate-
ness Maritain begins to bring his philosophical gifts to

bear on mystical contemplation. We saw in Chapter I his
concern for the concept and his insistence that the
concept is not what is known, but that by which the
object is known. The inner mystery of knowledge is the
union of knower and known by means of the concept, and
this union is not an entitative union as if we became
physically the thing we know, but rather an intentional
existence so that we become the other as other in a
spiritual existence which is the heart of the act of knowing.

But what of love? "If the immaterial activity of
knowledge is to become the other as other, the immaterial activity of love is to lose oneself in the other as the
self, to alienate myself in the reality of the other as
other to the extent that he becomes more me than I am
myself." (75) And he continues a little later: "The mystery of cognitive union and of the true compels the philosopher to conceive a 'being of knowledge' and an **esse
intentionale** which is not entitative being or being of
nature. The mystery of the union of love and of the good
compels him to conceive an **intentional being of love**
which is not entitative being either... In the spiritual
marriage the created will and uncreated love remain
entitatively distant to infinity, yet the soul, in its supernatural activity of love, loses or alienates itself in God
who, according to the being or actuality of love, becomes
her more than herself, and is the principle and agent of
all her operations." (76)

Maritain is now going to make some brief remarks of
the greatest significance for a deeper theology of contemplation, and he has a sense of the new ground he is
trying to break and modestly states: "The great Thomists
have admirably deepened and developed the questions
concerning the being of knowledge; fruitful principles for
a similar development concerning the intentional being
of love and the spiration of love can also be found in
their works." But it is Maritain, himself, who is going to
try to open for us this path. The immaterial existence
of love "is not an **esse** in virtue of which the one
(knower) becomes the other (the known); it is an **esse** in
virtue of which the other (the beloved), spiritually present
in the one (the lover) as a weight or impulse, becomes
him as an other self." (77) He continues in the next foot-

note: "...this presence is by mode of impulsion and
motion, and the beloved becomes the principle of action,
the 'weight' of the lover." (78)

When such highly charged remarks take place in Maritain's footnotes, they can be sometimes seen as an indication that a new insight is occurring to Maritain, for
he adds to these notes: "But this development itself is
still to be made." Further, it is highly likely that this
particular advance is taking place under the inspiration
of reading John of the Cross, and so it is a good example
of how while mystical contemplation does not enter into
the ontological constitution of metaphysics, it can certainly create an atmosphere in the spirit of the metaphysician which is conducive to deep metaphysical insights.

None of this union of love would be possible - and
here Maritain returns to his original question posed in
Chapter VI - without sanctifying grace and God's indwelling in the soul. But in the spiritual marriage this indwelling has become manifest through a union of love and the
gift of wisdom.

"Then the soul is in some manner the Whole, the very
infinity of God's life which erupts in it as if the whole
sea were to flow into a river, I mean a river of love
surging with vital operations and able from its very
source to become one single **spirit** with the sea." (79) Or
in more formal language: "the espoused soul loves and
gives by infinite love itself; it is by infinite love that the
soul operates according to the intentional being of love,
the while it operates according to the entitative being
by its own finite acts." (80)

All this is to say that in some mysterious manner the
soul begins to consciously participate in the inner life of
God as Trinity. "Essentially supraphilosophical, because
its proximate and proportioned principle is faith illumined
by the gifts, mystical experience tends from the beginning
to loving and fruitful knowledge of the three uncreated
Persons." (81) Supernatural contemplation is always, in
some fashion, an experience of the Trinity, but it is only
here in its culminating stage that it is experienced as
such. Therefore, Maritain will conclude: "This is the
reason why we believe that, no matter how high a mystical experience springing from a merely implicit super-

natural faith may rise outside the visible membership in the Church of the Incarnate Word, it never rises to this point." (82)

These chapters on mystical contemplation in the **Degrees** represent the high point of Maritain's systematic doctrinal elaboration of the topic. He will continue his deep interest in mysticism, but his output will shift to shorter occasional pieces that often have a more practical orientation. Nevertheless, he will continue probing the foundations of mystical experience, as we will see.

In 1938, as part of a series of nine lectures given in the United States, Maritain wrote "Action and Contemplation" which later appeared in **Scholasticism and Politics** in 1940. This tightly organized essay contrasts the Greeks' view of the superiority of contemplation over action - a superiority mixed with erroneous political consequences they drew from it, i.e., that most people lived to serve the few contemplatives - with the change of perspective that came with Christianity. "St. Thomas admits, like Aristotle, that considering the degrees of immanence and immateriality of the powers of the soul in themselves, intelligence is nobler than will, but he adds that considering the **things** we know and love, these things exist in us by knowledge according to the mode of existence and dignity of our own soul, but by love they attract us to them according to their own mode of existence and their own dignity, and therefore it must be said that to love things that are superior to man is better than to know them." (83)

Christian contemplation is not the privilege of the elite, but it is a call to women and men of every condition. This brings to his mind his earlier work on this call to contemplation and he feels that now theologians are coming to an agreement about this question: "...all souls are called, if not in a proximate manner, at least in a remote one, to mystical contempation as being the normal blossoming of grace's virtues and gifts." (84) And in reference to his "masked" contemplation where there is a predominance of the active gifts, he goes on to say: "It appears that the forms of contemplation to which souls faithful to grace will actually attain most often, will not be the typical one, where the supernatural

sweeps away everything, at the risk of breaking everything, but rather the atypical and masked forms I have
just mentioned, where the superhuman condescends in
some measure to the human and consorts with it." (85)
Each person is called, at least remotely, "to contemplation, **typical or atypical,** apparent or masked, which is
the multiform exercise of the gift of Wisdom, free and
unseizable, and transcending all our categories, and
capable of all disguises, all surprises." (86)

Finally, despite the catastrophe of World War II dark-
ening the horizon, Maritain is optimistic that the United
States, known world-wide for the "cult of action" has
"great reserves and possibilities for contemplation." (87)
This is a theme that will reappear several times in his
writings, for example, in the preface to his old friend
Pieter van de Meer's **White Paradise,** the story of the
Carthusian Order which is given to solitude and the
contemplative life. In a postscript to this preface dated
June 1952, he sees his prophecy beginning to be fulfilled
with the foundation of a Carthusian house in the state
of Vermont. An even stronger fulfillment could be seen
in the strong revival of monastic life in the United
States after the war in orders like the Trappists. Maritain, a man of many friends, corresponded with Thomas
Merton for 20 years starting shortly after the appearance
of Merton's **Seven Story Mountain.** In their yet unpublished correspondence which ranges over many topics
centering around the spiritual life, they touched on the
question of "masked" contemplation and Maritain's natural
mysticism.

In 1945, an essay by Maritain entitled "La dialectique
immanente du premier acte de liberté," (The immanent
dialectic of the first act of freedom), appeared in **Nova
et Vetera** and later appeared in his book **Raisons et
raisons** in 1947. This virtually uncommented upon essay
is one of Maritain's finest works, and it provides us with
a hidden key with which to delve deeper into the nature
of contemplation, not because it deals formally with
contemplation, but rather because it treats of the act of
faith which is so intimately connected to supernatural
contemplation.

Maritain takes as his starting point "any free act
through which a new basic direction is imposed upon my

life" (88), but for simplicity's sake restricts himself to
the first free act of a child which is not necessarily
remembered or even concerned with an important matter,
but nevertheless expresses a deep commitment. But what
is the inner dynamism of this act? In it the good is
chosen (or not chosen) precisely because it is good.
Therefore, this choice transcends the whole order of
empirical existence and it demands the existence of a
separate good. The act of choosing the good "tends all
at once, beyond its immediate object, toward God as the
Separate Good in which the human person in the process
of acting, whether he is aware of it or not, places his
happiness and his end." (89)

Thus, the child in "virtue of the internal dynamism
of his choice of the good... wills and loves the Separate
Good as the ultimate end of his existence" and "his intellect has of God a vital non-conceptual knowledge which
is involved both in the practical notion... of the moral
good as formal motive of his first act of freedom, and
in the movement of the will toward this good and, all
at once, toward the Good." (90) The will is going beyond
this or that particular good to the ground of all good
things "and it carries with itself, down to that **beyond,**
the intellect, which at this point no longer enjoys the use
of its regular instruments, and, as a result, is only
actualized below the threshold of reflective consciousness,
in a night without concept and without utterable knowledge." (91)

Further, if such a fundamental exercise of freedom
is to be efficacious and love God above all things, it
must be transformed and elevated by grace and charity.
This is due not only to the wounded condition of human
nature resulting from originial sin, but due, as well, to
the fact that the good which is the ultimate goal of all
good acts, "the only true end existentially" of human life,
is "God as the ultimate supernatural end," that is, God
in His very own life. So the whole order of good, since
it deals with what actually is, is concerned by that very
fact with men and women in a fallen and redeemed state
called to share in God's own life. Grace is always present
"to envelop and attract" us, and "our fallen nature is
exposed to grace as our tired bodies to the rays of the
sun." (92)

This kind of reasoning faces Maritain with a serious dilemma. If such a first act of freedom is a supernatural act that leads to a relationship of friendship with God, then it must somehow involve faith, for as St. Paul says: "Without faith it is impossible to please God; for he that approaches God must believe that He exists, and is the rewarder of those who seek Him." So Maritain's dilemma reads: This faith, according to St. Paul's words, cannot be implicit faith, but how can it be explicit in the case of a child who "does not even know that he believes in God?" (93) He resolves this impasse by avoiding the implicit-explicit dichotomy which deals only with conscious conceptual knowledge, and by invoking a knowledge that "reaches its object within the unconscious recesses of the spirit's activity" in which "the intellect knows in a practical manner the Separate Good **per conformitatem ad appetitum rectum** (through conformity to the right appetite) and as the actual terminus of the will's movement." (94) Under the light of grace, the good chosen becomes the good by which I shall be saved and the seperate good becomes God as savior. In short, the natural dynamism of the first act of freedom is transformed into a supernatural act and "under the light of faith, the right appetite then passes **in conditionem objecti** (into the sphere of objective actualization) and becomes, in the stead of any concept, the means of a knowledge which is speculative though escaping formulation and reflective consciousness... It is the movement of the will which, reaching beyond this good to the mysterious Existent it implies, makes this Existent become an object of the speculative intellect." (95)

But what has all this to do with our inquiry into Maritain's understanding of mystical contemplation? It reveals in a very striking way the kind of knowledge through connaturality that flourishes in supernatural contemplation. This knowledge coming through the first act of freedom "remains preconscious, or else hardly reaches the most obscure limits of consciousness, because, for one thing, it possesses no conceptual sign, and, for another, the movement of the will which brings it about is itself neither felt nor experienced, nor illumined and highly conscious as is love in the exercise of the gift of wisdom." (96) The knowledge coming through the gift of wisdom becomes conscious and experimental without being conceptual.

What we are seeing here is much more than the first free act of the child, for this first act of freedom is at once a supernatural act of faith and the beginning of the mystical life that is rooted in faith. The difficult theological issues that surround the nature of the act of faith can be best approached when we look at them from the perspective of knowledge through connaturality which links together this first act with its higher and more developed expressions. So while this knowledge coming through the choice of the good is not in itself mystical knowledge it "appears as an obscure preparation for and call to that experimental knowledge of God which is supernatural in its very mode of operation, and which reaches its highest degree in mystical contemplation." (97)

This essay affords us another intimate glimpse into Maritain's intellectual life. His great admiration for John of St. Thomas does not prevent him from seeing his limitations. Since faith demands a knowledge that God exists and that he rewards those who do good, then John of St. Thomas reasons that if someone like an uninstructed child is to have faith, God must send an angel or a preacher to them. Maritain observes: "The reason for this is that the great seventeenth-century theologian was, like all the scholastic doctors, interested in analyzing the objective requisites of the act of faith in themselves and in theologically elucidated terms rather than in looking for the psychological modalities in which they are realized in the experience of the subject. He consequently limited his study to the sphere of conscious thought and of conceptual or notionally expressed knowledge." (98)

We have arrived at a parallel situation to the one we saw in Chapter I in which Maritain moved from an objective consideration of the intuition of being to its subjective requirements. Now he realizes that the modern advance in psychological knowledge of the unconscious allows a more nuanced approach to the problem he is treating. Therefore, "at the moment when the concept of moral good is transfigured into that of the good by means of which I shall be saved, a mysterious reality pertaining to the supernatural order is actually revealed...

A new objective content is thus presented to the mind...
a knowledge in which the appetite 'passes into the sphere
of objective actualization' as John of Saint Thomas said
with reference to mystical knowledge.... Under the light
of faith the Savior-God toward Whom the élan of the
will moves has become the object of a nonconceptual
speculative knowledge which comes about through the
instrumentality of this very élan of the will." (99) There
is no need to demand explicit conceptual knowledge in
order for someone to come to faith because there is
another kind of knowledge that is "**formal and actual**
although it is preconscious." (100)

We are faced here with the fruit of Maritain's long
meditation on St. Thomas. He footnotes this page with
a passage from **De Veritate,** Question XIV, article 11, in
which St. Thomas is considering the possibility of someone
coming to faith who has grown up "in the forest or
among the animals" and so is without instruction. St.
Thomas reasons that this lack of explicit knowledge about
the content of faith could be supplied by God sending a
preacher or "through internal inspiration by which God
reveals those things which are necessary for believing."
Maritain, building on this comment, is explaining the
mode of this interior inspiration by a turn to the subject.
But this turn to the subject is not at all what many
modern philosophers understand by that phrase, but it is
a consideration of subjective requirements by someone
who is rooted as deeply as possible in the objective
metaphysical and theological demands of the question he
is dealing with. Maritain does not advance by overthrow-
ing St. Thomas or John of St. Thomas, but by situating
himself in the very heart of their doctrine and grasping
as firmly as possible the principles upon which it rests,
and then, ever so carefully, trying to make a new branch
appear on the old vine.

This attempt at a genuine development of the Thomistic tradition demanded that the subjective flow smoothly
from the objective and that Maritain deal first with the
tradition formulated as it was in objective terms and then
reflect on the subjective requirements of the issues at
stake. We saw in Chapter I that his detailed treament
of the metaphysics in **The Degrees of Knowledge** led
shortly thereafter to the breakthrough that appeared in

Sept Leçons. In this essay we can trace a similar process at work. Maritain's remarks on John of St. Thomas which appear in **Raisons et raisons** in 1947 in a subsection entitled "Theological Parenthesis" are absent in the original manuscript and in the 1945 **Nova et Vetera** article. Maritain wrote the original draft (preserved at the Jacques Maritain Center at Notre Dame) and then was inspired to break new ground by turning to the subjective demands.

The insertion of this theological parenthesis is one of the forerunners of a major shift in Maritain's thought. When he talks here of "the progress of psychological research with regard to the unconscious or preconscious life of the mind" (101), he is signaling a development that is going to become increasingly important in his study of mystical contemplation in the light of what he called the preconscious or unconscious of the spirit, or in regard to the supernatural order, the superconscious. Much later in a note on this essay in his **Church of Christ** he was to comment: "When I wrote this essay, I had not yet disengaged the notion of superconscious, so that the essay requires to be completed and corrected in this respect." (102)

Just what these terms preconscious and unconscious of the spirit mean for Maritain is to be found in his 1952 **Creative Intuition in Art and Poetry** and in **On the Grace and Humanity of Jesus.** In **Creative Intuition** he takes as his point of departure the modern psychological development of the unconscious, which means for him primarily the work of Freud. But for Maritain the Freudian unconscious is a deaf or automatic unconscious; it is "deaf to the intellect" and he conceives of the possibility of there being a spiritual unconscious or preconscious.

In a passage reminiscent of his preface to the 2nd edition of **La Philosophie Bergsonienne** he writes: "Reason does not only consist of its logical tools and manifestations, nor does the will consist only of its deliberate conscious determinations. Far beneath the sunlit surface thronged with explicit concepts and judgments, words and expressed resolutions or movements of the will, are the sources of knowledge and creativity, of love and supra-senuous desires, hidden in the primordial translucid night of the intimate vitality of the soul." (103)

It is not logic that rules in these depths below the surface of consciousness. In these deep reaches of the spirit are born insights, intuitions and the beginning of "intellectual knowledge... still unformulated, a kind of many-eyed cloud which is born from the impact of the light of the Illuminating Intellect on the world of images, and which is but a humble and trembling inchoation, yet invaluable, tending toward an intelligible content to be grasped." (104) But not all this stirring in the depths is meant to lead to discursive thought. There is "another kind of germ, which does not tend toward a concept to be formed, and which is already an intellective form or act fully determined though enveloped in the night of the spiritual unconscious." (105) This is the knowledge that expresses itself through the many pathways of connaturality, and we have seen one form of it surface in Maritain's essay, "The Immanent Dialectic." In this particular case Maritain has in mind poetic knowledge about which we must ask: "How can emotion be thus raised to the level of the intellect and, as it were, take the place of the concept in becoming for the intellect a determining means or instrumental vehicle through which reality is grasped?" (106)

In answer Maritain finds inspiration once again in John of St. Thomas', "Amor transit in conditionem objecti," which must find its analogous application to poetry. But if John of St. Thomas' doctrine on knowledge through connaturality can be applied to the origins of poetry, then conversely, the notion of the spiritual unconscious that Maritain is developing here can be applied to mystical contemplation. And the movement of Maritain's thought toward this application will dominate our attention for most of the rest of this chapter. Just how Maritain develops the theme of creative intuition in art and poetry will occupy us again.

In 1960, Jacques and Raissa's little book, **Liturgy and Contemplation,** appeared and though its principle aim was to examine the interrelationship of liturgy and contemplation, it treated once again of the typical and masked forms of contemplation. After quoting at length from their note IV in **De la vie d'oraison** on masked contemplation they go on: "We have just insisted on the diffuse

or disguised forms of infused contemplation. There is
nothing more secret - nor more important - than what
Father Osende, in a remarkable page of his book **Contem-
plata,** calls the prayer of the heart. It is through this
sort of prayer or contemplation, so silent and so rooted
in the depths of the spirit that he describes it as 'unconscious,' that we can truly put into practice the precept
to pray **always.** And is it not to it that Saint Anthony
the hermit alluded when he said that 'there is not perfect prayer if the religious perceives that he is praying'?"
(107)

They continue by quoting Fr. Osende to the effect
that while prayer of the mind requires our attention and
the "actual exercise of the faculties" and so cannot be
continuous, prayer of the heart, or 'unconscious' prayer,
can be continuous since it is a matter of love rather than
knowledge.

Later in 1966 with the appearance of **The Peasant of
the Garonne,** Maritain accused himself of having made
a "serious error" (108) in his treatment of masked contemplation in **Liturgy and Contemplation.** Once again in
the **Peasant** he asks himself how we can pray always and
he cites Fr. Osende on prayer of the heart, and this time
comments: "The prayer that Fr. Osende calls prayer of
the heart and that he describes as unconscious (it pertains to that 'supraconscious of the spirit' of which I
have said a great deal elsewhere) can and must, he says,
be continuous in the contemplative soul.' For we cannot
fix our minds on two objects at the same time nor continue to think always, whereas we can love always.' (at
least in the supraconscious of the spirit - only there, in
effect, can love be **in act** continuously). We are no longer
dealing simply with the vital impulse of prayer always
present **virtually** in consciousness; the prayer of the heart
itself remains in act - in the supraconscious of the
spirit." (109) We can see how the locus of contemplative
act is sinking down to what Maritain is calling the supra-
conscious of the spirit.

But what was the serious error that Maritain accused
himself of? "The prayer of the heart springs from the
supra-conscious of the spirit, but it is not at all 'masked'
contemplation; it is a typical **form** of contemplation, and
one of the most precious." (110) If Fr. Osende's descrip-

tion of prayer of the heart as 'unconscious' led Maritain
to equate it with masked contemplation, he now sees that
a typical form of contemplation can take place in the
unconscious, or better, supraconscious of the spirit. What
is at stake here is much more than a subtle refinement
of a minor point of mystical theology. It is a question
of Maritain's whole conception of the nature of contemplation which is undergoing a transformation as it is being
brought into relationship with the notion of the preconscious of the spirit, which in this case is elevated by
grace to become a supraconsciousness.

Just what is this supraconscious of the spirit? This
Maritain begins to work out in his 1967 **De la grâce et
de l'humanité de Jésus,** (On the Grace and Humanity of
Jesus). His starting point is another dilemma that surrounds the question of whether grace increased in the
humanity of Jesus. The Gospel according to St. Luke
seems to say yes when it describes Jesus growing in age
and wisdom and in grace. But St. Thomas seems to say
no, and Maritain attempts a reconciliation by distinguishing in the soul of Jesus a dimension in which he grew
in grace, and a superconscious dimension in which he
beheld the vision of God. If it was necessary for Maritain
to make a distinction before between the infraconscious
or Freudian unconscious and the preconscious of the
spirit, now in this little book he sketches some other
important distinctions. The divinized superconsciousness
of Christ is a consciousness of self in which Jesus experiences the Beatific vision, while our preconscious or
"natural supraconsciousness of the spirit does not constitute a transcendent **consciousness of self,**" but it is a
preconscious "secret sphere where in virtue of the supernatural gift of God is found the seat of grace, the beginning of eternal life." (111) These distinctions become
more tangible when Maritain takes the example of Fr.
Surin, a 17th century contemplative. Because of these
different dimensions of the spirit it was possible for him
to experience, in Maritain's opinion, mystical union in the
supraconscious of the spirit while being sorely troubled
by psychological problems in his infraconscious. And while
the world of the **"supraconscious divinized by the Beatific
Vision** could only occur in the unique case of the Word
Incarnate" (112), our own unconscious of the spirit,

through the grace of Christ, can become a supraconscious "that in certain souls a habitual union with God establishes itself, too profound to be perceived." (113)

The entry into the "path of contemplation" takes place "in a manner inaccessible to consciousness (in the depths of the supra-conscious of the spirit)" where the soul is "**habitually** aided by the gifts of the Holy Spirit." (114) And, as we saw, depending on which gifts predominate, there will be masked or typical contemplation. But the critical point for Maritain is that even if a typical form of contemplation is present in which the gift of wisdom predominates, it need not take the classic form found in John of the Cross and Teresa of Avila. Another possibility that very much interested the Maritains is what they called "contemplation on the roads", which is a contemplative call to Christians living in the world who thirst for a deeper life of prayer. In contrast to those people devoted to the active life who can partake of masked contemplation, these people are called to open contemplation. "But their path is a very humble one; it demands nothing but charity and humility, and contemplative prayer without apparent graces. This is the path of simple people; it is the 'little way' that St. Therese of Lisieux was in charge of teaching us: a kind of short cut - singularly abrupt, to tell the truth - where all the great things described by St. John of the Cross can be found divinely simplified and reduced to the pure essentials, but without losing any of their exigence. The soul is laid bare, and its very love-prayer as well - so arid at times that it seems to fly into distractions and emptiness... Sometimes, in a certain manner, this treasure is hidden from the soul themselves that possess it..." (115) Once again we see that the most difficult theological issues like the grace in the soul of Jesus is connected in Maritain's mind to the most pressing practical issues in the spiritual life, which in this case is the question of how contemplation might be given to people today.

He continues his examination of this subject by quoting at length from their **Liturgy and Contemplation:** "Saint Therese of Lisieux has shown that the soul can tend to the perfection of charity by a way in which the great signs that Saint John of the Cross and Saint Teresa of Avila have described do not appear... Let us add that in this contemplation on the roads whose development the future will doubtless see, it seems that constant attention to the presence of Jesus and fraternal charity are called to play a major role, as regards even the way of infused contemplative prayer." (116)

These last citations on contemplation on the roads have been from Maritain's **The Peasant of the Garonne,** and they are the closest he came to joining his reflections on mystical contemplation to his thought on the spiritual unconscious. Yet this encounter is of such importance that it is worthwhile for us to emphasize some of its major stages of development.

In the Maritains' 1924 **De la vie d'oraison** we saw how they nuanced the doctrinal statement of the normalcy of the call of all Christians to contemplation by introducing a distinction between typical and masked contemplation. There they distinguished: (1) a non-mystical contemplation like the contemplation of the philosophers, which is the culmination of the natural working of the faculties of the soul and a remote disposition to infused contemplation. (2) a masked contemplation in which the active gifts of the Holy Spirit predominate with a tempered or hidden exercise of the gift of wisdom, which gives to this non— mystical contemplation a certain savour of supernatural contemplation and is a proximate disposition to this infused contemplation. (3) And a contemplation which is the fruit of these other contemplations, but now aided more openly by the gifts of wisdom and understanding. This kind of contemplation is an ultimate disposition for infused contemplation and the anticipation of it. Implicit in all of this and, for that matter, in the work of the great Carmelite mystics, is an understanding that contemplation is, as John of the Cross puts it, not something we do with the faculties, but a gift passively received in the center of the soul. In more modern terms, contemplation is not something we do with our ego or even received there, but it takes place beyond ego consciousness, and is not always perceptible to the ego.

This brings us to the other current of Maritain's thought that we have been following that surfaced in his 1945 essay, "The Immanent Dialectic of the First Act of Freedom" that saw some of his first remarks on the spiritual unconscious. In fact, without putting the matter too strongly, it may be possible to trace the birth of this idea by examining the original manuscript and the nature of the 1947 insertion of the theological parenthesis. For example, the two sections that now bracket this parenthesis show significant reworking in the original manuscript, and much of this reworking has to do with the development of this idea of the spiritual unconscious. Section V, which now precedes this parenthesis, speaks of the "unconscious (inconscient) of the spirit" and anticipates the thought of the parenthesis, but its most subtle section on how right appetite passes "in conditionem objecti", and the comparison of this knowledge with the gift of wisdom are additions made to the original manuscript. In a similar way, the section that now follows the parenthesis shows additions that indicate a refinement of Maritain's thought on how conscious this knowledge coming through the first act of freedom is. Further, while the English translation of the 1947 essay shows the use of the word preconscious in the parenthesis in the form of the "unconscious and preconscious life of the mind", and "knowledge which is **formal and active** although it is preconscious," it also shows the use of the word preconscious in these other sections. However, when we go to the original text we find that in one case it is given as the rendering of the more general "inconsciente," while in the other it is a paraphrase for an original rendering which simply says "elle" and refers to "unconscious (inconsciente) and existential knowledge."

What I am suggesting is that we have in these alterations and additions a privileged window through which to see Maritain begin to develop the idea of the spiritual unconscious and apply it to a kind of knowledge that is very similar to mystical contemplation. Much later, he indicates in his **The Church of Christ** that this essay would have to be reformulated in the light of his further development of these ideas, which remark can be taken as a confirmation that his earlier essay was, in fact, an important starting point for this line of development.

It was not until 1960 that Maritain's thoughts on contemplation began to intersect with his ideas of the spiritual unconscious with the publication of **Liturgy and Contemplation.** However, as we saw, he identified masked contemplation with "unconscious" prayer. This was a

natural enough error, for masked contemplation evokes
the idea of a contemplation outside of consciousness more
readily than the typical or classical forms of contemplation that seem to be more perceptible and therefore to
be associated with consciousness. Further reflection made
it clear to Maritain that contemplation as such ought to
be seen in the light of the spiritual unconscious, and he
made his amends in **The Peasant of the Garonne.** In this
book he went on to begin to apply this contemplation
seen in the light of the spiritual unconscious, under the
heading of contemplation on the roads, to the important
problem of how contemplation is being experienced today,
which revolves around the central point of how much
Christians can expect to experience contemplation in
terms of consciousness.

While Maritain finally did join the spiritual unconscious
with his thought on contemplation, he was like a scout
who had gone exploring in an uncharted land and left
indications of some of the important landmarks without
having the energy and opportunity, because of his great
age, to cover the terrain in detail.

I would like to think that if Maritain had lived longer,
or come to this intersection earlier, we would have
another of his books, this one entitled, **Contemplation on
the Roads of the World,** (which, in fact, is the title of
a book that friends urged Raissa to write). In my hypo-
thetical version Maritain would have reformulated his
essay on the immanent dialectic, and gone on to make
a thorough examination of supernatural contemplation in
the light of the supraconscious of Jesus and conclude with
a more extensive treatment of how people today might
be experiencing contemplation.

As it is, Maritain has left us a milestone, albeit a
generally unrecognized one, in the 20th century renewal
of mystical theology. His work is a witness to the need
to bring the theology of contemplation into relationship
with the notion of the unconscious, but it also gives us
an eloquent testimony to the care we should have that
properly psychological notions stimulate seaching philosophical reflection on themes like the spiritual unconscious
or preconscious, which in turn become fitting instruments
with which to explore the riches of the Church's mystical
tradition.

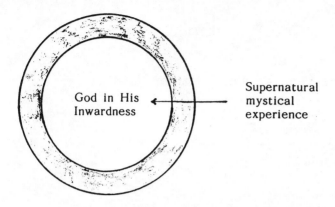

Now we come to our second diagram which attempts to depict supernatural mystical contemplation. What is at stake is no longer an indirect or analogical knowledge of God, but some sort of obscure yet real experience of God in his depths, an experience that comes through the inter-subjectivity of love. We no longer simply know that God must exist, but we experience His presence within us.

NOTES

(1) We Have Been Friends Together, p. 81.
(2) Ibid., p. 120.
(3) Ibid., p. 122.
(4) Ibid., p. 135.
(5) Notebooks, p. 43.
(6) Ibid., p. 36.
(7) Ibid., p. 37.
(8) Ibid., p. 42.
(9) Ibid.
(10) Ibid., p. 44.
(11) We Have Been Friends Together, p. 120.
(12) Adventures in Grace, p. 265.
(13) As cited in Adventures in Grace, p. 286.
(14) Antimoderne, Paris, Desclée, 1922, p. 250.
(15) As cited in Adventures in Grace, p. 286-287.
(16) Notebooks, p. 73.
(17) Henry Bars, "Maritain's Contributions to an Under-standing of Mystical Experience" in Jacques Maritain, The Man and His Achievement edited by Joseph Evans, New York: Sheed & Ward, 1963.
(18) Notebooks, p. 65.
(19) Bergsonian Philosophy and Thomism, p. 162.
(20) Ibid., p. 163.
(21) Ibid., p. 165.
(22) Ibid., p. 166.
(23) Ibid., p. 167.
(24) Ibid.
(25) Notebooks, p. 78.
(26) Raissa's Journal, Albany, New York, Magi Books, 1974, p. 31. Translated from Journal de Raissa, Paris, Desclée De Brouwer, 1963.
(27) Ibid., p. 35.
(28) Prayer and Intelligence, New York, Sheed and Ward, 1943, p. 22. Translated from De la vie d'oraison, Paris, St. Maurice, 1922, Rouart, 1924.
(29) Ibid., p. 23.
(30) De la vie d'oraison, p. 73.

(31) Ibid., p. 81.
(32) Ibid., p. 82.
(33) Raissa's Journal, p. 357.
(34) Ibid., p. 358.
(35) Ibid., p. 359.
(36) Ibid., p. 361.
(37) Réflexions sur l'intelligence et sur sa vie propre,
Oeuvres Complete, Volume III, p. 233.
(38) Ibid., p. 130.
(39) Ibid., p. 128.
(40) Ibid., p. 135.
(41) John of St. Thomas, The Gifts of the Holy Spirit,
New York, Sheed and Ward, 1951, p. 128, Dominic Hughes
translation.
(42) Preface to Bruno de Jésus Marie's, Saint John of the
Cross, London, 1932, p. xxv-xxvi.
(43) The Degrees of Knowledge, p. 8-9.
(44) Ibid., p. 249.
(45) Ibid., p. 249.
(46) Ibid., p. 249.
(47) Ibid., p. 250.
(48) Ibid., p. 252.
(49) Ibid., p. 260.
(50) Ibid., p. 259.
(51) Ibid., p. 260.
(52) Ibid., p. 262.
(53) Ibid., p. 264.
(54) Ibid., p. 272.
(55) Ibid., p. 277.
(56) Ibid., p. 277.
(57) Ibid., p. 283.
(58) Ibid., p. 315.
(59) Ibid., p. 311-312.
(60) Ibid., p. 314.
(61) Ibid., p. 315.
(62) Ibid., p. 325.
(63) Ibid., p. 325.
(64) Ibid., p. 327.
(65) Ibid., p. 338.
(66) Ibid., p. 338.
(67) Ibid., p. 339.
(68) Ibid., p. 349.
(69) Ibid., p. 350.

(70) Ibid., p. 356.
(71) Ibid., p. 356.
(72) Ibid., p. 358.
(73) Ibid., p. 362.
(74) Ibid., p. 364.
(75) Ibid., p. 368-369.
(76) Ibid., p. 369.
(77) Ibid., p. 369, note 5.
(78) Ibid., p. 369, note 6.
(79) Ibid., p. 372.
(80) Ibid., p. 373.
(81) Ibid., p. 378.
(82) Ibid., p. 381.
(83) **Scholasticism and Politics**, Garden City, New York, Image Books, 1960, p. 165.
(84) Ibid., p. 176.
(85) Ibid., p. 177-178.
(86) Ibid., p. 178.
(87) Ibid., p. 182.
(88) "The Immanent Dialectic of the First Act of Freedom, in **The Range of Reason**, New York, Charles Scribner's Sons, 1952, p. 66. Translated from **Raison et raisons**, Paris, Egloff, 1947. First version in **Nova et Vetera**, 1945 (20), p. 218-235.
(89) Ibid., p. 69.
(90) Ibid., p. 69-70.
(91) Ibid., p. 70.
(92) Ibid., p. 73.
(93) Ibid., p. 76.
(94) Ibid., p. 77.
(95) Ibid., p. 77.
(96) Ibid., p. 78.
(97) Ibid., p. 83.
(98) Ibid., p. 79.
(99) Ibid., p. 80.
(100) Ibid., p. 81.
(101) Ibid., p. 80.
(102) The Church of Christ, p. 261, note 23. De l'Eglise du Christ, O.C. Vol. XIII.
(103) **Creative Intuition in Art and Poetry**, Cleveland and New York, Meridan Books, 1953, p. 69.
(104) Ibid., p. 73.
(105) Ibid., p. 80.

(106) Ibid., p. 87.
(107) Liturgy and Contemplation, New York, Kenedy and Sons, 1960, p. 37.
(108) The Peasant of the Garonne, p. 228, note 103.
(109) Ibid., p. 228.
(110) Ibid., p. 228, note 103.
(111) On the Grace and Humanity of Jesus, New York, Herder and Herder, 1969, p. 49, note 2. Translated from De la grâce et de l'humanité de Jésus, Bruges, Desclée de Brouwer, 1967.
(112) Ibid., p. 80.
(113) Ibid.
(114) The Peasant of the Garonne, p. 230-231.
(115) Ibid., p. 234.
(116) Ibid., p. 235.

CHAPTER III

MYSTICISM OF THE SELF

If this book had limited itself to Maritain's natural mysticism, or as it is more commonly called today, his mysticism of the Self, it still would have been necessary to examine in detail both metaphysical and mystical contemplation. They form the indispensable context within which we can discover just what Maritain meant by natural mysticism.

Fortunately, instead of having to go back again to the beginning of the Maritains' life together, our story can begin in 1926. That was the year that saw the publication of "Mystical Experience and Philosophy" which, as I indicated in Chapter I, was to become, in a revised and augmented form, Chapter VI of **The Degrees of Knowledge**, dedicated to Garrigou-Lagrange. We looked at this chapter in some detail in our last chapter and saw Maritain denying emphatically that there could be an authentic mystical experience in the natural order. This was an answer demanded, he felt, by the fundamental distinction between nature and grace.

One of the objections to this denial that he poses reads: "There are Moslem, Hindu, Buddhist, and other schools of mystics. But the mystical experience to which they lay claim does not proceed from theological faith. There must, therefore, be a natural mystical experience." (1) And he answers that there can be authentic mystical experiences among other religions, but it comes from grace. These people "belong invisibly" to Christ's Church and have theological faith. Here he footnotes his discussion with a reference to St. Paul to the Hebrews and says they "cling with one's heart to the two primary truths in the supernatural order (a God exists who wills my salvation and who saves those who seek Him...) (2), and brings up the notion of implicit faith which was later refined in his "The Immanent Dialectic." The studies of men like Louis Massignon on al-Hallâj, he feels, confirms this general perspective from a factual point of view.

But if there are genuine cases of mystical experience among non-Christians, there are also dubious ones where "intense meditation and concentration, may present external resemblances to supernatural contemplation... (which) can stem from merely natural causes as well as higher influences. In these states the natural or philosophical 'contemplation' mentioned above undoubtedly plays an important role, but we do not think that for the most part it remains alone and in a pure state." (3)

He sees the possibility that "certain ascetic efforts, certain sequestrations of the soul exercised upon itself, can actually tend (unknown to the subject) towards a spiritual communication with angelic nature as such... the human mind would find itself giving way to the attraction, not so much of seeing pure spirits and seeking its happiness therein as receiving their help to be transported to a superhuman contemplation in which the soul would in some way mimic (in the suspension of consciousness, in a night, but as night different from the night of infused contemplation and the luminous cloud of Thabor) **their** way of knowing themselves and the highest." (4) We have arrived at a strong prefigurement of what is going to develop into Maritain's ideas on natural mysticism. The role of the angels will recede but certain key elements will remain, albeit in a transformed way.

Such an "intellectualist mysticism" seeks realization by means of "a completely metaphysical asceticism," examples of which can be found in certain Oriental schools. (5)

Maritain feels that the "Upanishads originally depend less on philosophy than on a contemplative source and a powerful intuition, more mystical than metaphysical, of the transcendence of the Supreme Being." But this "tremendous mystical striving... brings into play natural aspirations for perfect contemplation, and as natural harbingers of that contemplation, natural processes of asceticism and intuition which constitute in regards to it a stage of expectancy, as it were, and a metaphysic which aims at preparing the way for it..." (6) Here Maritain is concerned with demonstrating that there can be no natural mystical

experience along these metaphysical paths, but later when
the context has changed to creating an explanation of the
mysticism of India, then he will look at these same paths
with new eyes and discover their distinctive wonder and
mystery.

In 1929 Maritain had written an article called "Bergsonisme et métaphysique" which had appeared in the
Chroniques "Le Roseau d'or" and became in 1930 the
important preface to **La Philosophie Bergsonienne** which
we have encountered before. It touched on Indian thought
briefly and helps us see more clearly how his thoughts on
natural mysticism are evolving. In a manner similar to his
views on the practical science of contemplation that John
of the Cross created, he finds that the thought of India
is not so much a philosophy in the western sense, but
rather is shaped by its ultimate goal of deliverance:
"...from the very beginning, I mean from the fifth century
B.C., India did not take knowledge itself as its goal,
and... all its speculation is an ascetic discipline having
deliverance as its avowed or virtual aim." (7) It aimed not
at "knowledge pursued for its own sake, but exclusively
toward salvation." (8) Once this perspective is adopted we
can see how metaphysical thought in India "never gained
its automony" but was carried in the wake of its desire
for sanctity and "has chosen at all costs to transcend
human nature and reason." (9)

This effort at transcendence has at its limit "a be-
leaguering, a denaturing of man at the touch of pure
spirit, the kiss of the Angel... And of contemplation
itself, for which formlessness and **dissolvi** are not sufficient, whose whole is **esse tecum,** one will have realized
only the negative..." (10) Once again Maritain approaches
the threshold of the secret of mystical experience in
India, but the time is not yet ripe.

Somewhat later, in 1932, in a preface to the French
translation of G. Dandoy's work on the ontology of the
Vedanta, Maritain expands the development of these
thoughts and makes the links they possess with **The
Degrees of Knowledge,** which had just been published,
more explicit. Maritain was pleased that Fr. Dandoy had
expressed a view similar to the one that he had set forth
in his 2nd preface to **La Philosophie Bergsonienne** on the
goal of Indian thought not aiming at speculative know-

ledge, but deliverance. And Maritain comments that we are dealing with practical knowledge, but "it is not a question there of a practical knowledge clearly and typically differentiated like that of St. John of the Cross, but rather a vast movement of thought with a practical finality carrying with it all speculative effort of a theological and liturgical reflection which itself serves as the vehicle for powerful metaphysical energies." (11) Therefore, instead of following the laws of philosophy and starting from the basic facts that ground philosophical speculation, the philosophy of the Vedanta with which Fr. Dandoy is concerned follows the law of "religious contemplation and of the movement of the soul towards mystical union." (12)

This overriding finality has many implications. The Vedanta will not operate like a pure philosophy; it will lack "the metaphysical instrument of the analogy of being" and equate with nothingness the being which is not Being by itself. Even if certain of these formulations are deficient from a philosophical point of view, they are more accurate in terms of the practical mystical goal in question and "the interior experience to which it corresponds" can be an authentic contact with reality. (13) "If the self is declared identical to Brahma it is metaphysically speaking an affirmation of integral monism; and that can be a defective formulation, mystically speaking, of the experience of union." (14)

Further, "the subject-object problem beset both India and the West. In truth, far from the subject being all other than the object, as the Hindu schools assume, there are only **subjects** which, by the work of knowledge, are rendered **objects...**" (15) The subject is always ontologically deeper and thicker than the object and constitutes a "remainder" in relationship to it. "As well as we might know ourselves, there is always some obscurity in us about ourselves." (16) Pure spirits know themselves by their substance, but we know ourselves by our acts, and in knowing ourselves by our acts "it is the existence itself of our substance, it is the singular existence of our soul that we seize." (17)

In order to understand the full import of that last statement we have to go back to 1927 and pick up the thread of our story. That was the year when a young student began to appear at the Thomist Circle meetings at Meudon and stimulate Maritain to reflect more deeply on the mystical experience of India.

In that year Olivier Lacombe was attending the l'Ecole Normale Supérieure where he was soon to earn an agrégé in philosophy. Maritain encouraged him in his vocation as an indologist and he soon became an active participant at Meudon. Maritain's notes from these years read:

20th of January. Study meeting: Jacques de Monléon, Yves Simon, Olivier Lacombe...

Sunday the 23rd of February. Olivier replaces me at the Thomist meeting, he speaks on Buddhist logic.

7th of December (1930). Thomist meeting. Olivier on the Vedanta-Sara.

18th of January 1931. Thomist meeting. Olivier on the Baghavad-Gita. (18)

Just what role did Olivier Lacombe play in the formulation of Maritain's ideas on natural mysticism? When I asked him that question many years later he summarized his contribution as follows: "I was very young at that time and I was not in a position to do that (collaborate with Maritain in the creation of his philosophical thesis). I presented him with the Indian facts and he did the rest on his own." (19)

But just how did Maritain arrive at his conception of natural mysticism? In 1929-1930 Maritain had taken a sabbatical to work on the **Degrees of Knowledge** and it was towards the end of 1929, while he was revising Chapter VI, that he payed a visit to the noted Dominican theologian Ambrose Gardeil. Maritian had been impressed by Gardeil's **La Structure de l'ame et l'experience mystique,** and the book served as a catalyst for Maritain's insight into the nature of the mysticism of the Self.

Once Maritain had this inspiration he visited Fr. Gardeil again a few months before his death on October 2, 1931, curious, I think, to see what he would make of such a novel use of his book on Christian mysticism. Fr. Gardeil had not thought of such an application, and I imagine he was somewhat mystified by the whole idea. Sometime in late 1931 or early 1932, in the form of a fifth appendix to his **Degrees of Knowledge** entitled, "On a Work of Fr. Gardeil," he wrote down the kernel of his insight.

For Maritain, **La Structure** was one of the "most

notable contemporary attempts" to examine mystical experience from a speculative point of view and in a rigorous fashion. But there were several points that he felt needed further discussion. The most important of these, from the perspective of natural mysticism, concerned the human soul's knowledge of itself. Gardeil had postulated that the "soul's habitual or radical knowledge of itself, inasmuch as it is a spirit, is **partly actualized** in its reflections on its acts." (20) Maritain thought that this was mistaken, for as long as the soul is united to the body this kind of knowledge is hindered.

What he would prefer is to see the soul's radical knowledge of itself as spirit as the metaphysical foundation for our ability to reflect upon our acts which gives rise to our self-awareness. This distinction is critical for Maritain's views on natural mysticism. We have no direct spiritual vision of our soul, yet when we reflect upon our acts of knowledge we know them to be our own. This self-reflection is no intuitive vision of our essence, but rather is an experimental knowledge that "belongs to the **purely existential order** and implies the presentation to the mind of no other **quid** than my operations reflexively perceived in their emanation from their principle." (21) Thus without having any vision of ourselves we do have an existential experience of ourselves, an experience of the singular existence of the soul.

Maritain then gives us the substance of his insight:

"We might add that this could be the starting point of a possible interpretation of certain natural states imitating or prefiguring authentic mystical experience. It is not impossible that a certain natural mysticism could apply itself methodically to the stripping off of particular images and representations, in the hope that, on the verge of the unconscious, as Bergson would say, it might achieve an evanescent grasp of the pure existence (unsignifiable in itself) of the soul's substance. But (supposing that the beginnings, at least, of such an experience were possible) since no content of the "essential" order, no **quid** would in any event be attained, it is patent that in these circumstances philosophical thought reflecting upon these attempts would inevitably run the risk of confusing the self ("atman") with the supreme Principle." (22)

Thus in a highly condensed way Maritain gives us the

essential nucleus of his theory of natural mysticism, and
it will be the task of the rest of this chapter to explore
its meaning and look at some of its implications. But first
it is worthwhile to once again emphasize Maritain's intellectual style. When, in 1929, he had revised chapter VI
of the **Degrees** and talked to Fr. Gardeil, he must have
felt something tugging at his intuition that he could not
yet articulate. He is putting the final touches on the
Degrees of Knowledge when it dawns on him that not only
do Fr. Gardeil's views on the soul's transparency to itself
need revision, but they point to a deeper understanding
of the Indian mystical experience. If there is no intuitive
vision of the soul of itself, there is a very precious
experimental knowledge we have of ourselves, and could
not this existential knowledge be a door that leads to
some sort of contact with the Absolute? In short, Maritain
has this powerful new intuition as a fruit of his effort
to complete his monumental **Degrees of Knowledge**, and
by an irony of the creative process, at the very moment
he has taxed himself to finish his work, a new beginning
appears. But this insight is too new and too radical to
immediately find its full articulation. That is going to
have to wait another six years.

It was also typical of Maritain, that while during the
course of 1931, when he was working on this insight,
which at first glance seems so highly intellectual and
removed from ordinary existence, he was at the same
time considering becoming part of a Christian ashram. At
Jacques' urging, Raissa, in the fall of 1931, had taken up
her journal again. It was an extremely busy time at
Meudon, and her entry for October 3rd reads: "Jacques
has drawn up a ukase destined to protect us against the
invasions of our fellow men! We will try once again, and
see if it is possible for us to continue to live at Meudon
without losing any leisure for prayer..." (23) These constant demands probably formed part of the context within
which a Christian ashram with time for solitude and
prayer would appear very attractive.

During this same time Raissa was reading Romain
Rolland's **Vie de Ramakrishna** in which he cites Gandhi,
and Raissa is led by his words to reflect on the contemplative life among Catholics: "...our religious communities
ought all to be more contemplative than they are." (24)

And in an entry for October 24th: "Does God want us to leave here to have greater solitude? Or to have greater solitude without going away? I no longer know what I want in my heart of hearts... Going away would be a great adventure!" In late November Jacques talks with Dom Florent Miège who advises them against their ashram project.

During those years he continued to be presented with the facts of the religious experience of India:

Sunday the 13th of March. Thomist meeting. Olivier brings Mlle Ramakrishna.

Sunday the 7th of January. Thomist meeting, tiring. Jacques on the object and objectivity; Olivier on Ramanuja. (25)

In 1937 Lacombe was to write an article entitled, "Sur le yoga indien" which appeared in the **Etudes Carméli-taines,** and publish his **L'Absolu selon le Vedanta,** and Maritain was to write of him to his friend John Nef at the University of Chicago on November 8, 1938: "Olivier Lacombe is the best and most dear of my students; he is someone completely superior and I recommend him in an unconditional manner which is rare." (26)

Finally, on September 21-23, 1938 at the Fourth Congress on Religious Psychology held at Avon-Fontainbleu Maritain fully expressed his intuition in a talk entitled, "L'experience mystique naturelle et le vide" (Natural Mysticism and the Void). It was published in Etudes Carmélitaines the following month and appeared in his book **Quatre essais sur l'esprit dans sa condition charnelle** in 1939.

In this essay Maritain characterizes mystical experience as "a possession-giving experience of the absolute." This is a wider definition than equating mystical experience with supernatural contemplation, and it leaves the door open to considering the possibility, not of a naturally attained supernatural mystical experience, but a natural mystical experience. Such a natural mystical experience is not to be confused with the natural philosophical contemplation of Chapter I: "Is this natural contemplation of divine things a **mystical experience** in the natural order? I believe not." (27) The reason it is not is because this philosophical contemplation, despite the affective overtones that can accompany it, knows God at a distance through the mirror of creatures; it knows God in and through the intuition of being that makes use of concepts. But can there be a natural mystical experience, a kind of "metaphilosophical contemplation" that is the result of a deeper and more religious desire, not just to know that the cause of creatures exists, but to embrace and contact in some way this source of being? Mystical experience wants to do this. It wants to go beyond concepts and experience the absolute by a kind of knowledge that Maritain calls "nescience, of possession-giving not knowing." And this mystical knowledge can be divided into two types depending on the kind of connaturality that it involves. The first is a mystical experience by means of affective connaturality which is the supernatural contemplation of Chapter II. The second is mystical experience by an intellectual connaturality, "a natural contemplation which by means of a supra or para-conceptual intellection attains a transcendent reality." (28) This is a metaphilosophical contemplation that reverses rather than continues the normal direction of philosophical contemplation by achieving its knowledge at the price of the elimination of all concepts.

Maritain's starting point for exploring this natural mysticism is the knowledge that we have of ourselves, "the inner and obscure experience of myself, through myself." (29) Inspired by Ambrose Gardeil's book he realized that although there cannot be even a "partial actualization of the latent self-intellection of the soul reflecting upon itself," (30) this self-knowledge can become an invaluable entranceway to a genuine natural mystical experience. Our self-awareness is a "true experience of the singular existence" of the soul in and through its operations. (31) But this awareness of our existence does not directly reveal to us "what" we are. We know this what only in a piecemeal fashion by making use of our concepts. In contrast, our experimental knowledge of ourselves is a "purely existential" knowledge. However, this existential knowledge is usually intimately commingled with our discursive activities, but now Maritain envisions the possibility of a deliberate and determined effort in which spiritual seekers, like the sages of India, would concentrate on this primordial fact of their existence and eliminate every image and distinct operation of the mind.

By means of this negative act, "an act of supreme silence," they would try to penetrate this experience of existence to its depths and finally come to a state in which "the soul empties itself absolutely of every specific operation and of all multiplicity, and knows negatively by means of the void and the annihilation of every act and of every object of thought coming from outside - the soul knows negatively - but nakedly, with veils - that metaphysical marvel, that absolute, that perfection of every act and of every perfection, which is **to exist**, which is the soul's own substantial existence." (32)

Laying aside every what or essence, they descend into a silence which is "a negation, a void, and an annihilation which are in no sense nothingness." (33) Instead, this very void becomes the formal means by which they know, not an intuitive vision of the soul, but its very existence which seems to surge up and be a gift passively received. Instead of supernatual contemplation's amor transit in conditionem objecti, in this natural mysticism "vacuitas, abolitio, denudatio transit in conditionem objecti" (voidness, annihilation and denudation become the formal means by which the object is known.) The abolition of all acts becomes the supreme act, and it is this emptiness that becomes the way in which "the deep fathomless 'to exist' of subjectivity" is negatively experienced as a "mystical experience of the Self." (34) But if this experience of the existence of the soul can only take place by the elimination of all essences, then "it is comprehensible that this negative experience, in attaining the existential **esse** of the soul, should at the same time attain, indistinctly, both this same existence proper to the soul and existence in its metaphysical amplitude, and the sources of existence." (35) "And how could this experience, being purely negative, distinguish one absolute from the other? Inasmuch as it is a purely negative experience, it neither confuses nor distinguishes them. And since therein is attained no content in the 'essential' order, no **quid**, it is comprehensible that philosphic thought, reflecting upon such an experience, fatally runs the danger of identifying in some measure one absolute with the other, that absolute which is the mirror and that which is perceived in the mirror. The same word 'atman' designates the human self and the supreme Self." (36)

In short, the very powerful yet obscure experience of
our own existence can become the doorway through which
we can pursue, not the path of essence, but that of existence to the very bedrock of the human spirit which is
our very existence as it comes forth from the source of
existence. But this existence is known through the medium
of emptiness so that there is no way to distinguish the
existence of the soul, the existence of all created things
and the existence which is God. All of this will remain
incomprehensible if we have not understood that metaphysics is supremely alive and lives principally not in words
but in the intuitions that give birth to them. This is not
Maritain trying to make some academic evaluation of
Hindu mystical experience, but rather trying to awaken
us to the riches of the metaphysics of St. Thomas that
can allow us to begin to see into the dark yet luminous
depths of natural mystical experience.

Maritain, in an important footnote to this discussion,
finally completes the journey that he had started back in
the **Degrees,** and clarifies the relationship between the
experience of the existence of the soul and the experience
of God: "It is the substantial **esse** of the soul which is
the object of (negative) possession; and by this negative
experience of the self God is attained at the same time
without any duality of act, though attained indirectly...
God being known (1) by and in the substantial **esse** of the
soul, itself attained immediately and negatively by means
of the **formal medium** of the void; (2) in the negative
experience itself of that substantial **esse** (just as the eye,
by one and same act of knowing, sees the image, and in
the image the signified) -, all this being the case, I think,
it is permissible in such an instance to speak of a
'contact' with the absolute, and of an improperly
'immediate' experience (that is to say, one wrapt up in
the very act of the immediate experience of the self) of
God creator and author of nature." (37)

Maritain now realizes that what he wrote in The
Degrees of Knowledge, as far as a natural experience of
the depths of God is concerned, ought to be maintained,
but his position of natural mysticism can be nuanced
further: "But here we have an experience of God **in**
quantum infundens et profundens esse in rebus (insofar as
He is pouring in and infusing existence in things), in-

directly attained in the mirror of the substantial esse of the soul... God, without being Himself an object of possession is attained by this same act of the experience of the self..." (38) There is, then, such a thing as "a negative mystical experience of the **presence of immensity**" and the **Degrees** has to be corrected in this regard, and he carried this out in the postscript to the third edition dated July 25, 1939 in which he states that this essay completes chapter VI.

This profound insight into natural mysticism will remain from now on one of Maritain's fundamental intuitions, and he will continue to refer to it, but at the same time he will not formally try to advance and deepen it; there is not going to be another essay devoted exclusively or chiefly to this theme. He will write, for example, in his 1938 essay, "Action and Contemplation": "Natural spirituality has techniques which are well determined and are, moreover, good and useful." (39) And in a more powerful passage he indicates that the East, even in the temporal order, looks to this natural mysticism, while in the West supernatural contemplation has remained in the sacred order. "If a new age of Christian civilization should dawn, it is probable that the law of contemplation superabounding in action would overflow in the secular and temporal order. It will thus be an age of the sanctification of the profane." (40) Much later, in the **Peasant of the Garonne,** he comments that although Thomism has fallen out of fashion, it is "actually in pretty good shape. In saying this, I am thinking of its intrinsic development and of the various kinds of research it has stimulated. I have in mind particularly the progress which is owed to it (thanks to the investigations of Olivier Lacombe and Louis Gardet) in the understanding of Oriental thought (and a good understanding, too, with its representatives) and in an authentic theory (the only one) of natural mystique." (41) Still later in **Approches sans entraves** he will remark in passing on the role that natural mysticism played in the philosophy of Heidegger.

His **Approches to God,** published in 1953, is one of the few places where he devotes more than a passing glance to natural mysticism. In a discussion of a potential "sixth way" by which to demonstrate the existence of God, he speculates on how natural mystical experience

may have originated in places like India. This sixth way
is based on an intuition that is reminiscent of Maritain's
comments in the **Degrees** on the philosopher who is led
to the existence of God by a reflection on his own
thought. Here it arises in the form of a sudden penetrating insight: **"(H)ow is it possible that I was born?"** (42)
"...(H)ow is it possible that that which is thus in the
process of thinking, in the act of intelligence, which is
immersed in the fire of knowing and of the intellectual
grasp of what is, should once have been a pure nothing,
once did not exist? (43)

This is an intuition that arises from the very transcendence of the mind in relationship to sense and imagination, space and time; could this fire of consciousness
and thought have once been nothing? "Yet I know quite
well that I was born." (44) And once we struggle with this
dilemma we may arrive at its resolution: "It must have
been in a Being of transcendent personality, in whom all
that there is of perfection in my thought existed in a
supereminent manner, and who was, in His own infinite
Self, before I was, more than I myself, who is eternal,
and from whom I, the self which is thinking now, pro-
ceeded one day into temporal existence." (45)

Maritain had this insight "entirely independent of any
contact with Indian thought," (46) but he realized that a
similar intuition could have arisen in India, and if subse-
quent metaphysical reflection on it had been inadequate
it would have given rise to a confusion "between the
divine Self and the human self." (47)

In 1956, a revised and augmented version of **Quatre
essais** appeared. As far as Maritain's essay on natural
mysticism is concerned, the changes were confined principally to the addition of some footnotes. They ranged from
an acknowledgement of the role of Lacombe and Gardet
during the intervening years in developing these ideas and
references to some of Maritain's later works. The most
extensive of these new notes was added to the final page
of the essay and deals with the question of whether grace
can give natural mystical experience "a participation in
the supernatural union of charity." More precisely it asks
whether natural mysticism can be a valuable aid for the
interior life of the Christian, and it comes in the form
of a quote from Olivier Lacombe. Lacombe thinks that

the answer must be reserved (réservée), but historically speaking it is possible to come to a more positive judgment. "We do not see why a soul that is upright and consequently habituated and moved by a hidden grace would not be able to live a particularly rectified yoga as a vicarious exercise of an authentic spiritual life." (48)

It is becoming clear by now that Maritain did not devote much energy to the applications of his theory of natural mysticism or even to developing its theoretical side further, but as this footnote indicates, he was not unaware of some of the interesting avenues that would have to be explored. He left the application of his work in the able hands of his friends Olivier Lacombe and Loius Gardet, as we have seen. Gardet, a student of Islam, wrote widely on comparative mysticism in works like his **Expériences mystiques en terres non chrétiennes** and La **Mystique.** But it is his 1972 study, Etudes de **philosophie et de mystique comparées,** that is particularly important for our examination of Maritain's thought.

Lacombe, for his part, continued to add to his earlier works with volumes like his **Indianité,** which contain an article on Ramana Marharshi, and he produced in collaboration with Gardet a work that expounded in masterly fashion the hints contained in Maritain's original essay. This book, **L'Expérience du Soi,** has been in the works since the late 1950's and excerpts had appeared in the **Revue Thomiste** in 1968, 1972, and 1976, with the book finally appearing in 1981.

In this volume Lacombe deals with the Vedanta and yoga, while Gardet deals with Islamic mysticism, modern poetry and Heidegger. But what interests us here are their theoretical reflections on Maritain's natural mysticism. Lacombe characterizes it not as "a metaphysical intuition contemplating the intelligible riches of the essence of the soul," but as "an inward looking ecstasy or enstasy (entase) of the act of knowing in the act of existing." (49) This is an immediate but negative experience of the self, and the creative presence of God is experienced, not directly - for that would be the same as supernatural mystical contemplation - but "mediately in the mirror of the Self." (50) It is "a quasi negative experience of the presence of immensity." (51)

But if this experience of the self has played such a

powerful role in the religious life of India and Islam, it
must represent a fundamental possibility for the human
spirit in its present condition, and so wouldn't it be
reasonable to expect to see it appear in Western thought,
as well? Gardet pursues this possibility, not only with a
chapter on poetry and Heidegger, but by discussing atypical forms of this experience of the self. They range from
spontaneous cases of cosmic consciousness to various
mixtures of natural and supernatural mysticism which can
take place in two directions. In the first, a natural mysticism can be touched and transfigured by supernatural
contemplation, and in the second, a Christian mystic can
experience moments of natural mysticism and this, in
Gardet's opinion, seems to have been true in the case of
Meister Eckhart.

Despite the strong metaphysical character of the
experience of the self, Gardet is careful not to confuse
it with metaphysics as a philosophical discipline, for one
works by the negation of all concepts while the other
through concepts. Therefore it is important not to see "in
the (negative) grasp of a transempirical 'I', a metaphysical intuition of being." (52) While both the experience of
the self and the intuition of being originate in the spiritual preconscious of the soul, and while they can vitally
influence each other, they unfold in distinctively different
ways. If the experience of the self takes precedence, as
it does in India, then it will "guide and center" metaphysical reflection. (53) And the result will be quite different
than a metaphysics founded on the eidetic intuition of
being. The non-conceptual nature of the experience of the
self, when it becomes an object of reflection, will make
it extremely difficult to distinguish philosophically the
human self in its deepest roots from the divine Self.

Maritain realized that since all people are called to
grace, and therefore to supernatural contemplation, then
there was no need to deny that there could exist situa-
tions in which "a sort of **composition** of the upward
movement of Yoga and of the disciplines of natural
contemplation of the Self combined with supernatural
touches and the love of charity," and that they could
"come to impart to the natural mystical experience a
higher value and a participation in the supernatural union
of love." (54) Building on this thought Lacombe asks

himself again whether the experience of the self can serve as a preparation for the supernatural life of contemplation. And he answers in much the same words as he did before: "We do not see the reason why an upright soul drawn along by the dynamics of the universal vocation of humanity to a supernatural life in God, conditioned, elevated and activated by a secret grace, could not be able to live a particularly rectified discipline of yoga as a vicarious exercise of spirituality..." (55)

Gardet, looking at this question from a slightly different perspective, sees the possibility that in the context of grace and aiming at a supernatural union with God, certain techniques similar to those that lead to the experience of the self could play a role in the spiritual life as long as the technique does not "invade the whole soul," (56) and substitute a belief in the efficacy of the technique for a humble waiting on grace.

In his **Etudes de philosophie et de mystique comparées** Gardet, in commenting on Maritain's essay, looks carefully at Maritain's footnote on the way God is experienced in natural mysticism. We have seen that for Maritain this natural mysticism has as its object the substantial existence of the soul. But two difficulties have to be avoided. If we say that we experience God directly, even in his creative presence by immensity, we are, in fact, claiming to have a supernatural mystical experience on the natural order, for there is no distinction in God between God as Trinity and God as creator, even though there is a distinction from our point of view. As Gardet puts it: God, the ineffable One and Three, is his presence of immensity..." (57) But if we turn around and say that we only experience God through his effects, we have to be careful that we don't lose sight of the testimony of India which talks about the experience of atman as the absolute, as well as the experience of atman as the soul.

So Maritain will talk about the experience of God by and in the esse of the soul, an experience that takes place "immediately and negatively by the formal medium of the void," or an "improperly immediate" experience; it is an experience "indirectly attained in the mirror of the substantial existence of the soul," or "a negative mystical experience of the presence of immensity itself." Gardet comments: "We ought to be extremely guarded

here in the vocabulary employed. It is not the creative
influx in itself that is attained by the experience. It is,
we believe, even necessary to say: that it is not God in
the presence of his immensity who is attained experimen-
tally, but the effect of this presence in a singular existence. Let us say, if you want, that it is, indeed, the
creative and conserving act of God, but in and by its
terminus ad quem. So although God the author of nature
is thus experienced, it is not only indirectly but also
mediately: by the medium that remains such, the substantial **esse** of the soul. There would be some risk of confusion to speak here of an 'immediate' experience even
if it is 'improperly immediate'." (58)

Even though in the experience itself there can be no
distinction made between the existence of the soul and
God as the author of existence, it still remains true that
"every singular existence only realizes itself as limited
by essence," (59) and "the experience of the presence of
immensity of God remains mediate, the substantial existence of the soul - although not seized as limited, since
no conceptual context enters into play - guards its function of **medium;** it is a pure existence (pur exister) which
is directly attained, but not pure existence (l'exister pur),
pure act." (60)

The refinements of Gardet are worth considering, but
they should not diminish our sense of the immediacy and
the absolute character that the actual experience of the
self has, which is what I think Maritain is trying to cap-
ture. If we have a direct though negative experience of
the existence of the soul, and this existence is in direct
contact, radiant as it were, with the inpouring of existence coming from God, and if, in the night and void of
all concepts the two are experienced as one, then we can
understand Maritain's "improperly immediate." As long as
we maintain the fundamental distinction between nature
and grace, supernatural mysticism and the mysticism of
the self, we have some room in which to grope towards
the best form of expression for this natural mysticism.

Later, the application and extension of Maritain's ideas
was continued by his companion in the Little Brothers of
Jesus, Heinz Schmidt. Today, unfortunately, this extremely
valuable way in which to come to grips with the growing
encounter between Christianity and Eastern religions is

neglected with the exception of a few people like Yves
Floucat in his **Vocation de l'homme et sagesse Chrétienne**
(61) or Louis Chamming's, the Parisian follower of Maritain.

The work of this Maritain school of the mysticism of
the self has examined many facets of the question, with
the notable exception of Buddhism. Here Buddhism's insistence on the limits of philosophical understanding, the
non-substantial character of all things, and its non-theistic
viewpoint have made such an application more difficult.
This has combined with the limited nature of the Buddhist
texts available to Maritain and caused him to say in his
Church of Christ that Buddhism is led: "to reject absolutely all substantial being: neither God, nor soul, the
experience of deliverance is an experience of the non-
existence of the self." (62)

In another place he comments: "And this changes many
things. I noted a moment ago that in the Hindu experience... the soul attains in night the pure **esse** of the self.
Now such an act, in which the reality of the self culminates, is clearly out of the question, since there is no
self... It seems indeed that what is required can be only
a total vanishing of the spirit. And one does not experience the vanishing of the spirit." (63) And he concludes
concerning Buddhism: "It would indeed be futile to seek
there unfathomable metaphysical depths." (64) This negative evaluation, I think, he would have revised had he had
a chance to study the rich collection of Mahayana and
Tibetan Buddhist texts that have become available in
recent years, as well as the moving testimony of modern
accounts of Zen Buddhists who have undergone awakening
experiences, for it is abundantly clear from them that the
experience of no-self and emptiness is not simply privative
or negative, but supremely positive, so that Buddhism, in
its highly distinctive way, can be said to illustrate
another facet of the mysticism of the self. To change
Maritain's phrase: the experience of the non-existence of
the self is - by the kind of paradox so dear to the old
Zen masters - the means by which the Self is experienced
as Non-Self or Emptiness.

In chapter I we saw the transition from an objective
consideration of the intuition of being in the 1932
Degrees of Knowledge to a more subjectively oriented
treatment in the 1934 **Sept leçons.** In chapter II we traced

an analogous movement into the depths of the subject
through the various versions of his essay, "The Immanent
Dialectic," in which the idea of the unconscious or preconscious of the spirit began to emerge. Now we have to
ask ourselves whether it is possible to discern a similar
process of development, a move to a deeper awareness
of subjectivity, in Maritain's ideas on natural mysticism.
I believe that it is, but here, since he left so much of
the application of these ideas to others, the trail is
fainter. For example, in chapter X of **The Church of
Christ** - which has a preface dated June 11, 1970 -
Maritain is speaking of how people belong invisibly to the
Church. And he has in mind particularly the members of
the great non-Christian spiritual families of Hinduism,
Buddhism and Islam. And when he tries to explain how
they could belong to the Church without any conscious
knowledge of Christ, he makes use of the ideas he developed in his immanent dialectic essay. He footnotes this
discussion with the comments we have seen in chapter II:
this essay ought to be corrected and completed by being
reworked in the light of the supraconscious of the spirit.
What we are seeing, then, is a conjunction of the idea
of belonging invisibly to the Church, natural mysticism
and the supraconscious of the spirit, although Maritain
does not systematically explore the many implications of
bringing these ideas together. It is possible, however, to
pursue this implicit theme in Maritain's thought by looking
at his ideas of subsistence and subjectivity.

   This story starts in 1932 with appendix IV of **The
Degrees of Knowledge** entitled, "On the Notion of Subsistence." Maritain wants to situate the difficult notion of
subsistence in the context of what he considers St.
Thomas' most fundamental metaphysical insight, the application of the Aristotelian doctrine of potency and act to
the relationship between essence and existence. There is
a relationship of potency to act between a faculty and
its operation, but when we come to the case of essence
and existence, Maritain sees a transcendence of existence
in relationship to essence. Essence which is "completely
achieved in its line of nature" is in potency to a whole
other order which is existence. Essence does not receive
existence as if it somehow preexisted existence, and existence was "a determination of that potency's own reserves

of determinability" (65); "...existence is not the achievement of essence in the order of essence: it does not form
part of the order of essence..." (66) Put in another way:
"Existence is not a quiddatative determination... By a
unique paradox, it actuates essence and it is not an
actuation of the reserves of potency within essence." (67)

But how can this transcendence be bridged so that
essence can make existence its own? It needs "to be
terminated on the side of existence, face to face with
existence, in such a fashion that it **cannot** be joined to
another substantial essence in order to receive existence."
(68) And this termination is a substantial mode which is
subsistence itself which is neither the quiddatative aspect
of essence nor existence. In short, subsistence becomes
the way in which essence already achieved in the quiddatative order is made ready to actually exist; it bridges
the transcendence of existence in relationship to essence.
"Thus, subsistence appears as a sort of individuation of
the essence **with respect to the order of existence,** leaving the line of nature to face up to something altogether
different, to make the leap into existence." (69) If essence
is a closed whole in the quiddatative order, it needs to
become a "closed whole **in the order of the aptitude to
exist...**" (70) Then **"it is not that by which a man is what
he is,** it is **this man, you** or I..." (71)

While this appendix represented a continuation of the
typical Thomistic approach, it did not rest completely
easy on Maritain's mind. In 1947, in his **Existence and the
Existent,** in a chapter entitled, "The Existent" and devoted
to subjectivity, he took another look at subsistence. When
examining these views we should keep in mind that this
book was being prepared while Maritain was developing
his ideas on the preconscious of the intellect between
1945-1947.

The subject is "that **which** has an essence, **that which**
exercises existence and action..." (72) But once Maritain
has summarized the argument of appendix IV, he begins
to break new ground. God doesn't create essences. God
creates existents, subjects, and we "shall never know
everything there is to know about the tiniest blade of
grass or the least ripple. in a stream." (73) We know
subjects "by achieving objective insights of them and
making them our objects; for the object is nothing other

than something of the subject transferred into the state
of immaterial existence of intellection in act." (74) Each
of us is a deep well of subjectivity and each of us "is
situated precisely at the centre of this world." (75) We
are not objects to ourselves but subjects, and we are
"confronted with subjectivity as subjectivity." (76) Our
previous explorations of Maritain's thought have prepared
us to understand him when he continues: "I know myself
as subject by consciousness and reflexivity, but my substance is obscure to me." This brings to mind his reflections on the work of Gardeil that prepared the way for
his theory of natural mysticism. Then he links this insight
with the experiences that give rise to the intuition of
being: "When a man is awake to the intuition of being he
is awake at the same time to the intuition of subjectivity; he grasps, in a flash that will never be dimmed, the
fact that he is a self, as Jean-Paul Richter said." He
concludes by linking subjectivity and intuition of being
with natural mysticism: "The force of such perception may
be so great as to sweep him along to that heroic asceticism of the void and of annihilation in which he will
achieve ecstasy in the substantial existence of the self
and the 'presence of immensity' of the divine Self at one
and the same time - which in my view characterises the
natural mysticism of India." (77)

In itself "the intuition of subjectivity is an existential
intuition which surrenders no essence to us... Subjectivity
as subjectivity is inconceptualisable." (78) Yet there are
ways in which we can know the subject as subject. In the
first of these ways subjectivity "is felt as a propitious and
enveloping night" that surrounds all our inner activities;
it is a formless and diffuse knowledge which in relation
to reflexive consciousness, we may call unconscious or
pre-conscious knowledge." (79)

In addition to this unformed knowledge of subjectivity
that envelops all our activities there is a more definite
kind of knowledge of subjectivity that comes through
connaturality. There is, for example, supernatural mystical
knowledge in which love that becomes "the formal means
of knowledge of the divine Self, simultaneously renders
the human self transparent in its spiritual depths." (80)
Maritain could have gone here and added that among
these kinds of connatural knowledge is the knowledge of

the existence of the soul that takes place through the
void of all concepts. Could not this, too, be taken as a
knowledge of subjectivity, but in darkness?

Maritain has seen that starting from our experience
of our subjectivity we can arrive at a sense of the interiority of being, the richness and fecundity of existence
that superabounds in knowledge and love, in what he calls
"the generosity of being." (81) The implications of this
primordial experience of us being present to ourselves can
be pursued in different directions. In one case it might
give rise to the eidetic intuition of being and a keen
sense of God's existence. In another we might be driven
to grasp the root and the source of our being as deeply
as possible, and leaving all distinct knowledge behind,
come to the mysticism of the self. And in a third situation this obscure but vibrant experience of subjectivity
and our sense of a prisoner in our own interiority where
no one seems to be able to enter can make us grasp that
supernatural contemplation would be a great liberation in
which we would transcend the limits of our subjectivity
by experiencing the subjectivity of God, not through
concepts but through charity. It is of the very nature of
love to reach out to the other precisely as other, to aim
at their very subjectivity whether it is the case of human
love or divine love. In these kinds of love, albeit in different ways, "the intellect within us becomes passive as
regards love, and, allowing its concepts to slumber, thereby renders love a formal means of knowledge (and) to this
degree we acquire an obscure knowledge of the being we
love similar to that which we possess of ourselves; we
know that being in his very subjectivity... by an experience of union." (82) This passage and this whole chapter,
in fact, is a fitting crown to Maritain's footnote in the
Degrees of Knowledge on the nature of love that we saw
in chapter II.

In 1954 Maritain wrote a revision of his appendix IV
of the **Degrees.** It was occasioned by the preparation of
a new English translation of the book, a project that
pleased him very much, for he felt the old translation
lacking and it had omitted the appendixes altogether. This
new appendix gave him an opportunity to deal with some
objections that had been raised against the old version.

The first had made subsistence a way in which to

overcome the transcendence of existence in relationship
to essence. But it is probably fair to say that this transcendence had originated in a perception of essence that
had stressed its completeness on a quiddatative level and
failed to fully grasp that the deepest intelligibility of
essence was its existability. I have been at pains to indicate the central role Maritain played in putting existence
in the center of the 20th century Thomistic revival, and
this is but an illustration of how it slowly had to filter
into the traditional way of explaining subsistence. Essence
is this or that capacity for existence, and the more that
is recognized the less need is there to try to find a way
to join essence to existence; if essences are certain
capacities for existence, then in a very deep way essence
already belongs to the order of existence. Therefore in
his 1954, "On the Notion of Subsistence" Maritain insists
that, first of all, it is "existents that we experience" and
we derive essences from them.

"In the second place, essence is in potency to existence, to the act of existing, which is act and perfection
par excellence... In the third place, there is an intuition
of existence" in which "esse is perceived quite precisely...
as an **exercised** act... as an activity in which the existent
itself is engaged, an energy that it exerts." (83) It was
this distinction between existence as received and existence as exercised that Maritain had not brought out in
his first version. Since essence is in potency to existence,
it "suffices by that very fact to limit, appropriate or
circumscribe to itself the existence that it **receives.**" But
where then is the role of subsistence? "But to **exercise**
something besides bare essence is necessary, namely the
supposit or person." (84) There is still a transcendence of
existence in relationship to essence but now Maritain will
draw another inference: "essence or nature can **receive**
existence only by **exercising** it... In other words, it can
receive existence only on condition of being drawn at the
same time from the state of simple essence and placed
in an **existential state** which makes it a **quod** capable of
exercising existence." (85)

In a similar way existence is not "received by the
essence as in a pre-existing subject which would already
be in existential act." (86) But again the inference to be
drawn is the same as before. Since existence must be an

exercised act - something cannot truly be without exercising existence - essence can receive existence only by
exercising it. So subsistence becomes, not a way of making the essence incommunicable, but of placing it in a
"state of exercising existence." (87) Now Maritain can
invoke the old scholastic axiom that causes are causes of
each other. Existence can be received by the essence only
if the essence exercises existence. "In other words, it is
by being received by the essence that existence is exercised by the supposit, and it is by being exercised by the
supposit that existence is received by the essence." (88)
And in a passage that throws new light on his natural
mysticism he comments: "If it can be said that the supposit actively exercises existence, it is in the more profound sense - and this is the privilege, and the mystery
of the act of existing - that for esse, to actuate the
supposit is (in virtue of the divine action compenetrating
it) to be the fundamental and absolutely first activity of
the supposit in its substantial intimacy and depths - activity eminently its own when the supposit is a person -
by which it is other than nothing." (89)

Maritain continues this new appendix with a theological discussion on subsistence in Jesus which we need not
go into except for one striking point. Just as appendix V,
"On a Work of Father Gardeil," contained an insight that
was to flower in his essay on natural mysticism, this 1954
appendix has a passage that will be developed in 1968 in
his On the Grace and Humanity of Jesus: "And according
as He was man that which pertained to His state as
comprehensor was reserved, so to say, for heaven by
reason of the exigencies of His state as viator." And the
philosophical underpinnings of this statement are Maritain's views on the supraconscious: "We ask ourselves, or
rather we ask theologians, if the conclusion to be drawn
from this is not that the supreme evidence that Christ,
in His human soul, had of His own divinity by the beatific
vision did not pass into the experience of Himself proper
to the homo viator in the form of only an absolute certitude or knowledge which was sur-conscious or super-con-
scious (I mean retained at the supreme spiritual point of
consciousness), and neither signifiable in concepts nor
communicable?" (90)

It is reasonable to suppose that Maritain's ideas on the

preconscious of the intellect were fresh in his mind,
having given his Mellon lectures on creative intuition
in art and poetry in 1952, which were later produced in
book form in 1954, and it would have been natural for
him to transfer these thoughts developed in relationship
to art and poetry to the theological realm when the
occasion arose of preparing this new appendix. The appendix was orginally written in French and the original
manuscript is at the Jacques Maritain Center in Notre
Dame. It shows less alterations than some of his other
manuscripts, but exhibits an interesting hint of the same
struggle we saw in the various versions of "The Immanent
Dialectic." In the passage just cited on sur-conscious or
superconscious knowledge, the original shows considerable
reworking, and significantly lacks the word sur-conscious
and the parenthesis: "I mean retained at the supreme
spiritual point of consciousness."

But what does this exploration of the admittedly difficult notion of subsistence have to do with natural mysticism? At the end of chapter II we surmised that if
Jacques had continued his work on supernatural contemplation he would have increasingly viewed it in the light
of the preconscious of the spirit, and I like to think that
he would have followed a similar process in regards to
his theory of natural mysticism.

This would have been a continuation of Maritain's role
of suffusing the objectively oriented Thomistic tradition
of the past with a deeper appreciation of subjectivity. Put
in another way, if traditional Thomism had placed a
certain stress on essence, and developed a particular
notion of subsistence in order to address the fundamentally existential character of St. Thomas' metaphysics,
then Maritain can be seen as completing this traditional
approach of subsistence by emphasizing its relationship to
existence and subjectivity.

Set in this context, if Maritain's natural mysticism
were developed in the light of subjectivity, then it would
make Thomism better able to engage in the growing
dialogue with Eastern religions where an inward looking
orientation predominates. Maritain's explanations of subsistence, precisely because they flow from the mainstream
of Thomistic metaphysics, advance that tradition without
losing any of its treasures. If consciousness and objective

requirements of knowledge were long to the forefront, Maritain is showing the limitations of conscious logical knowledge and the connections it has with the spiritual unconscious. Such an approach is much more congenial to the spiritual universe of the East - not to mention many modern people of the West - which has devoted itself to trying to fathom the realms beyond the ego and building a philosophy on the basis of non-conceptual experiences.

There pain and suffering lead to the pursuit of the source of existence which is found beyond all concepts or essences in a night where the existence of the self, and in and through it, the Divine Self, is experienced. But if no conceptual knowledge is possible in this experience itself, then is it possible to call the experience of the self an experience of subjectivity? If this means an experience of the inwardness or the subjectivity of God, the answer is no. But if it means a contact with something richer and deeper than any concept or object - let us say with a subject, but not known as a subject - then we can begin to grasp that it is an experience of subjectivity in the sense of the deepest roots of the human subject and in and through it the presence, in darkness and the void, of the ultimate Source and Subject. There is no experience of God as person, but neither can we say that it is a non-personal or non-subjective experience. The very experience is not nameable, not subjective, not objective, not personal, not impersonal.

When Maritain writes, "If it can be said that the supposit actively exercises existence, it is in the more profound sense... that for esse, to actuate the supposit is (in virtue of the divine action compenetrating it) to be the fundamental and absolutely first activity of the supposit in its substantial intimacy and depths..." can we not understand this in relationship to natural mysticism? The ego, in the metaphysical sense, is far distant from the supposit or person. The person in its deepest center, in the heart of the spiritual unconscious, is where it receives all its actuality, its existence directly from the hand of God; it receives its very to be by exercising it. It is not enough for us to receive existence, for to truly possess it we must exercise it, and so subsistence is no different from the existent itself, the essence precisely as exercising existence. We are subjects with an immense interiority which is the interiority of existence itself superabounding in knowledge and love, and too often our very depths are hidden from us.

But if someone, driven by suffering and attracted to these depths, were to leave aside all concepts and travel through this void to the very existence of the soul, what would that be like if not but an experience of our deepest subjectivity where we exercise existence, and in that very existence receive all that we are from the hand of God? But in a night where no concepts can enter, the existence of the soul and the existence of all things and the existence of God are all experienced together. Maritain's exploration of subsistence, then, holds the promise to peer more deeply into the metaphysical depths of the mysticism of the self.

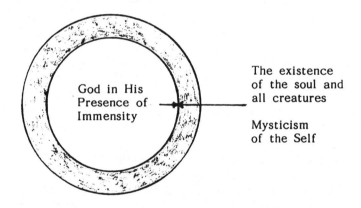

God in His Presence of Immensity

The existence of the soul and all creatures

Mysticism of the Self

We come now to our third and final diagram. We go beyond the face of essence and reach the very foundation of the soul, its very existence, and in and through that existence, God the source of all existence. This experience is neither an eidetic intuition of being, nor an experience of God in His inwardness. We could say it is mystical in mode since it is an actual experience of God as absolute, yet it is metaphysical in content, for it is an experience of God as the author of existence through emptiness.

NOTES

(1) The Degrees of Knowledge, p. 272.
(2) Ibid., p. 273, note 2.
(3) Ibid., p. 275.
(4) Ibid., p. 276.
(5) Ibid.
(6) Ibid.
(7) Bergsonian Philosophy and Thomism, p. 39.
(8) Ibid., p. 40.
(9) Ibid., p. 41.
(10) Ibid.
(11) "Commentaire au livre de G. Dandoy, L'Ontologie du Vedânta," in Oeuvres Complètes, Vol. IV, p. 1061.
(12) Ibid., p. 1062.
(13) Ibid.
(14) Ibid., p. 1062-1063.
(15) Ibid., p. 1064.
(16) Ibid.
(17) Ibid.
(18) Notebooks, Chapter 5.
(19) Videotaped interview, May 1990.
(20) The Degrees, p. 445.
(21) Ibid., p. 447.
(22) Ibid.
(23) Raissa's Journal, p. 201.
(24) Ibid., p. 202.
(25) Notebooks, Chapter 5.
(26) As cited in the Notes et Documents of the Institut International "Jacques Maritain", 1980, p. 2, from a letter dated February 10, 1951.
(27) "The Natural Mystical Experience and the Void" in Understanding Mysticism edited by Richard Woods, Garden City, New York, Image Books, 1980, p. 478.
(28) Ibid., p. 483.
(29) Ibid., p. 485.
(30) Ibid.

(31) Ibid., p. 486.
(32) Ibid., p. 489.
(33) Ibid.
(34) Ibid., p. 490.
(35) Ibid., p. 491.
(36) Ibid., p. 492.
(37) Ibid., p. 499, note 18.
(38) Ibid.
(39) "Action and Contemplation" in **Scholasticism and Politics**, p. 178.
(40) Ibid., p. 181.
(41) The Peasant of the Garonne, p. 139.
(42) **Approaches to God**, New York, Harpers, 1954, p. 73.
(43) Ibid., p. 74.
(44) Ibid., p. 75.
(45) Ibid., p. 76.
(46) Ibid., p. 82-83.
(47) Ibid., p. 83.
(48) "L'Experience mystique naturelle et le vide" in **Quatre essais sur l'esprit**, Paris, Desclée de Brouwer, 1956, p. 163, note 23.
(49) L'Experience du Soi, Paris, Desclée du Brouwer, 1981, p. 161.
(50) Ibid., p. 169.
(51) Ibid., p. 170.
(52) Ibid., p. 194.
(53) Ibid., p. 203.
(54) "The Natural Mystical Experience and the Void", p. 495-496.
(55) L'Experience du Soi, p. 170.
(56) Ibid., p. 238.
(57) Etudes de philosophie et de mystique comparées, Paris, J. Vrin, 1972, p. 164.
(58) Ibid., p. 164.
(59) Ibid., p. 165.
(60) Ibid., p. 166.
(61) Paris, Editions Saint Paul, 1989.
(62) On the Church of Christ, p. 123.
(63) Ibid., p. 97.
(64) Ibid., p. 98.
(65) The Degrees, p. 430.
(66) Ibid., p. 431.
(67) Ibid.

(68) Ibid.
(69) Ibid., p. 433.
(70) Ibid.
(71) Ibid.
(72) Existence and the Existent, p. 70.
(73) Ibid., p. 74.
(74) Ibid.
(75) Ibid., p. 75.
(76) Ibid., p. 76.
(77) Ibid.
(78) Ibid., p. 76-77.
(79) Ibid., p. 77.
(80) Ibid., p. 78.
(81) Ibid., p. 89.
(82) Ibid., p. 90.
(83) The Degrees, p. 436.
(84) Ibid.
(85) Ibid., p. 437.
(86) Ibid.
(87) Ibid., p. 438.
(88) Ibid., p. 439.
(89) Ibid.
(90) Ibid., p. 443.

CHAPTER IV

THE ESSENTIAL AND THE EXISTENTIAL

In this chapter we are faced with three tasks in order to complete our understanding of the three contemplations: (1) We have to see more clearly how these contemplations interact and influence each other. (2) We need to situate Maritain's metaphysical and mystical work more precisely in his own times. (3) We need to place him in the larger panorama of the history of Thomism and try to deepen our understanding of his inner intellectual and spiritual inclinations.

(1) In the first three chapters we have concentrated principally on Maritain's comment that these three contemplations "of themselves and by essence... are totally different." But this is just one half of his lifelong project to distinguish in order to unite, or in this context: "These three types of contemplation are able, in fact, in this or that person, to give rise to different mixtures." (1) In short, if these contemplations are in themselves distinct they all can dwell within us and influence and interpenetrate each other.

The foundation for examining this interplay among the three contemplations can be found in Maritain's fundamental distinction between the essential and the existential, a distinction that is already implicit in his "to distinguish in order to unite." In the Degrees he is constantly delineating the essential characteristics of the various sciences in terms of their various epistemological types in order to map the terrain of the one mind and to trace the dynamic interrelationships that grow up between the various sciences.

This theme of the essential and the existential was to become more explicit around the time he was writing the Degrees, for it coincided with a running debate on the possiblity of there being a Christian philosophy which

involved Bréhier, Gilson, Jolivet, Blondel and others.
Maritain's contribution to this discussion appeared in
several articles in 1932 and in **De la philosophie chrétienne** in 1933. For Maritain, while it would be a mistake
to speak of a Christian philosophy that would have a
specifically Christian content - for then it would not be
a philosophy, that is, a work of human reason - this does
not mean there cannot be a Christian philosophy in
another sense. This would be a philosophy that takes root
and grows in the mind and heart of the Christian and far
from being shut off from this Christian life, is nourished
and guided by it. This Christian life does not supplant the
work of reason, but strengthens it. In Maritain's language
there is a vital distinction between the "order of specifi-
cation and the order of exercise," or between "nature"
and "state." "This means that we must distinguish between
the **nature** of philosophy, or what it is in itself, and the
state in which it exists in real fact, historically, in the
human subject, and which pertains to its concrete conditions of existence and exercise." (2) He continues a little
later: "Christian philosophy is philosophy itself in so far
as it is situated in those utterly distinctive conditions of
existence and exercise into which Christianity has ushered
the thinking subject, and as a result of which philosophy
perceives certain objects and **validly demonstrates** certain
propositions, which in any other circumstances would to
a greater and lesser extent elude it." (3)

The light of faith aids the light of reason to see its
own objects more clearly. And if metaphysics can in this
sense be called Christian, the situation of moral philosophy is even more acute. Moral philosophy has the task
of elucidating the goal towards which we should strive.
But this end is not a purely natural one; the good that
we seek is the supernatural goal of union with God. This
leads Maritain to what he calls moral philosophy adequately considered. "Man is not in a state of pure nature,
he is fallen and redeemed. Consequently, ethics... in so
far as it takes man in his concrete state, in his existential being, is not a purely philosophic discipline." (4) If
in speculative philosophy the object was natural and the
light of faith aided us to attain it more fully, here in
the realm of practical philosophy, the object itself is
beyond the range of unaided human reason, and so reason

must depend on faith for its knowledge of it.

This fundamental distinction between the essential and the existential has been emerging, as well, in our treatment of the evolution of Maritain's thought on each of the three contemplations. In Chapter I we saw him move from an analysis of the nature of being in **The Degrees of Knowledge** to a consideration of the subjective requirements of the intuition of being in **Sept leçons.** Maritain had realized that it was not enough to talk about the objective nature of being. No matter how true such an analysis is it has to be supplemented by an examination of how, in the actual circumstance in which we live, we can attain this insight. And this is all the more true because existence itself is not principally a matter of essence, but of actually existing subjects. In chapter II we saw a similar situation emerge. The world of logically manipulated concepts makes up just part of the human spirit. There is, in addition, a spiritual unconscious that plays a primordial role in the exercise of our intellects. And in chapter III Maritain's ideas on natural mysticism point the way to this same spiritual unconscious and to experiences that take place beyond concepts.

What we are faced with in this distinction between an essentialistic analysis and an existential evaluation, or as Maritain puts it, between nature and state, is another situation analogous to his intuition of being. Like the intuition of being it has to do with essence and existence and a fundamental insight that is so simple that it is difficult to grasp, and which has concrete approaches to it. We might be led to it, for example, by pondering some moral question that resists us until we realize that the complete answer cannot be found at the level of the rational nature of things, but must take into account the fallen-redeemed state of the human race. Or it might come from struggling with a problem in the spiritual life, like the call to contemplation, just as Maritain did. No matter how much infused contemplation can be demonstrated to be the normal outcome of the development of the virtues and the gifts of the Holy Spirit, our analysis is incomplete until we look at the concrete state in which men and women strive to reach this contemplation. Then we can be led to such notions as Maritain's masked contemplation, and later his development of the idea of the spiritual unconscious.

In a similar fashion, the reason why philosophical demonstrations of the existence of God like those of St. Thomas leave so many people cold and unconvinced is not to be found principally in any weakness of his metaphysical reasoning, but rather in more existential considerations. These ways pointing to the existence of God, no matter how correctly stated, derive their intellectual force from the intuition of being, which in turn is effected by our fallen-redeemed state. And this state which is a supernatural one makes us long for a union with God that comes through grace so that our metaphysics, while being essentially complete, can be existentially unsatisfying. Human nature as human nature has no efficacious desire for divine union. Human nature in the concrete, transformed by grace, does.

If metaphysics of itself does not have to look to mystical experience for its completion, the individual metaphysician does, and inversely, the life of faith of this philosopher can nourish the metaphysical enterprise. How could someone who tried to draw close to God in faith and by begining to enter the ways that lead to supernatural contemplation fail to be influenced by this supernatural union when they turned to metaphysical contemplation? In such a situation the metaphysician would be led - if he or she were not paralyzed by a false fear of faith conflicting with reason - to see the object of this metaphysical contemplation more clearly and be strengthened in the pursuit of it.

Not only does the light of faith know God who is the object of metaphysical contemplation in a higher way, and thus fortify our metaphysical insight, but it also helps to heal the ravages of our intellectual insight brought about by original sin. When St. Thomas talked about the effects of original sin, he directed most of his remarks to its moral consequences. Maritain, in contrast, at the end of his life, reflecting on what he called an existential epistemology, tried to develop the thought of St. Thomas by looking at how original sin effected the intellect. In his essay, **Réflexions sur la nature blessée**, (Reflections on wounded nature), he tried to show how original sin dimmed our primordial intellectual insights like the intui-

tion of being. In the state of original justice, grace in
"the supra-conscious of the spirit" through the infused
theological virtues "enlightened and fortified reason" not
in its nature, but "in its natural exercise." (5) With the
loss of original justice the equilibrium of the natural
working of reason was disturbed, and to illustrate what
happened Maritain created a metaphysical typology in
which each of the cardinal virtues corresponds to a particular aspect of the work of doing metaphysics. Prudence
is associated with a "solidité rationelle" which has to do
with the organization of concepts. Justice is connected
to a "justesse du verbe" which is clearly saying what is
seen, while fortitude is attached to a "hardiesse de
regard" by which Maritain means intuitive insight. Finally,
temperance is linked with a "limpidité de la pensée" in
which the thoughts of the philosopher are expressed without distortion by any unconscious pressure of imagination
or emotion. At first glance such a schema may appear
to be rather artificial, but it takes on solidity as Maritain
continues by looking at the history of metaphysical
thought in this perspective. This is not some typology
that Maritain dreamed up and now wants to impose on
whatever material he finds at hand, but rather it has
emerged for him out of his pondering the vicissitudes of
the metaphysical enterprise. It is worth noting, as well,
that this brief excursion into typology is another of
Maritain's attempts to balance metaphysical analysis with
more concrete and existential considerations. There is
even a more personal note concealed here, for Maritain
singles out intuitive insight and the organization of concepts for special attention and these were, in fact, two
qualities that he excelled in.

   In each metaphysician, with the equilibrium coming
from original justice gone, one of these qualities will
predominate over the others. Why? "Because the psychological temperament (attention, I don't in any way understand by this the unconscious pressure of subjectivity, I
understand the **native constitution of each person**) is not
only varied among the diverse individuals of the species,
which is completely normal, but, by the loss of original
justice, holds reason itself in a certain dependence in its
regard, and because even among the greatest philosophers
the intelligence feels the repercussion of the psychologi-

cal temperament." (6)

Maritain will go on in this essay and indicate more precisely how the lower powers of the soul like the imagination impact on the intellect and effect its ability to see. But what is critical for us to note is that if the heaven of the soul is restored by grace, then these disturbances due to temperament and the excessive autonomy of the lower powers of the soul will lessen and metaphysical insight will become keener. It will be in a contemplative soul like that of St. Thomas' that the light of the intuition of being will dawn, not because it is a supernatural light in itself, but because grace has begun to restore the distorted and cramped dimensions of the soul, allowing space for this insight to germinate. In this context, Maritain, with another nod to the work of Lacombe and Gardet, adds that this same process can take place among non-Christians and give rise to a genuine perception of the intuition of being. (7)

The light of faith effects the light of metaphysical understanding, not by violence, but by "a natural and spontaneous movement like that of the tides and the seasons." (8) Here Maritain turns once again to John of St. Thomas who likens this kind of illumination to what transpires between the angels. The higher light of faith "irradiates... the object which on an inferior plane belongs to the specific field of philosophy" so that the natural light of reason is strengthened by a "real motion or impression deriving from the habitus of faith" passing into it. (9) "In the same way," writes John of St. Thomas in his **Cursus Theologicus,** "the light of the superior angel strengthens and perfects the intellectual potency of the inferior, proposing to it the object illuminated in a higher way... " (10)

If the intellect can be moved by this higher light, the will can be equally attracted by a deeper goal that grace has made known to it. Love makes the intellect more keen to penetrate the mystery of being, and to go beyond the intuition of being in quest of that knowledge through love that is supernatural contemplation.

If Maritain as a philosopher devoted his energy primarily to examining how the light of reason could be aided by faith, theology and contemplation, he was not unaware that this process worked both ways. In St.

Thomas, for example, metaphysical wisdom was perfected by dwelling in a soul given to prayer and contemplation, but this perfected metaphysics was brought into the service of theology. Maritain realized that Thomas' conception of theology was not one in which reason explored revelation, as if the light of reason were the supreme light that theology saw by, but rather the light of faith took up reason in order to try to articulate the mysteries transcending reason that it adhered to by this higher light. These two lights are so intimately connected in the theological enterprise that Maritain, after the pattern of his moral philosophy adequately considered, conceived how philosophy could become a research worker for theology. In such a situation philosophy would be awakened to problems that had arisen in theology, and explore them in a properly philosophical fashion, not to arrive at theological conclusions which would be impossible, but to open new philosophical paths which might not only enrich philosophy itself, but also be of service to theology, as well. For examples of this kind of procedure we can look to Maritian's **On the Grace and Humanity of Jesus,** and some of his essays in **Approches sans entraves.**

Philosophers and theologians have struggled over the interrelationships of reason, faith, theology and supernatural contemplation for a long time, and no doubt will continue to do so. But at least they are on familiar ground. In contrast, when we come to the mysticism of the self, relationships with the metaphysics and supernatural contemplation have just begun to be explored. Maritain, after his original essay, left the matter in the hands of Lacombe and Gardet, and we have looked at their remarks in chapter III.

The practitioners of the mysticism of the self live in the same fallen-redeemed world as Christians do and are called to the same goal. If we apply Maritain's careful analysis in the "Immanent Dialectic" to these men and women who have made heroic efforts to leave all concepts behind and join themselves to the absolute, then we can see that these efforts aimed at natural msyticism can become transformed by grace and serve to draw them to divine union. This is the conclusion that Olivier Lacombe reached and which Maritain approved by citing it in his 1956 version of his essay on natural mysticism. While it is true that any good act is capable of a similar transformation, the mysticism of the self has a privileged position, for it is a question of men and women striving to discover the ultimate meaning of life.

But what of the relationship between this natural mysticism and metaphysical and mystical contemplation? If metaphysical contemplation is unsatisfying in an existential sense, if it can increase our thirst for the vision of God, is it not possible that if this thirst were experienced in a non-Christian context it could give rise to a natural mysticism? Then these men and women yearning for a living contact with the absolute would seize upon metaphysical insights and their radical inadequacy and conceive the bold plan of going beyond all concepts and against the natural direction of the working of the intellect in order to assuage that thirst. The result could be a mysticism of the self in which philosophy is seen as too tame and too ineffectual, and what is born is a natural mysticism, a heroic dedication to attain the absolute using every power of mind and body. It is clear that in such a situation metaphysics would no longer culminate in a philosophical contemplation, but would become a post-experience reflection on the natural mystical experience. And as Maritain indicated, such a reflection would tend to identify the existence of the soul, God as the source of existence and the existence of all things.

But this does not mean that the mysticism of the self could not serve to strengthen metaphysical insight and contemplation. The interior attitudes that Maritain describes as prerequisites for the intuition of being like an active and attentive silence or a deep immersion in the very actuality of things could be cultivated by means of eastern forms of meditation. And if the archfoe of a genuine Thomistic metaphysics is a scholasticism fixated on concepts, then here, too, non-conceptual forms of meditation could loosen the hold of this conceptualism and allow intuitive insight to take its rightful place. This is not the place to explore these kinds of possibilities; it suffices that we recognize that the light of the mysticism of the self could strengthen the light of the intuition of being in a way analogous to how the light of faith fortifies metaphysical insight. If the mysticism of the self is an actual experience of God in and through the existence of the soul, then how could it fail to quicken the instinct of metaphysics for the author of existence?

Inversely, metaphysics could help the practitioners of this natural mysticism see that there is a difference between the non-conceptual experience of the self and certain post-experience conceptualizations that have become closely attached to it. Then it would be possible for them to examine afresh the relationships among the existence of the soul, the existence of things and the One Who is existence without a limiting essence.

The relationship between mystical contemplation and natural mysticism holds equally fascinating possibilities. Mystical contemplation could illuminate in a higher way the very object that the mysticism of the self pursues in its own fashion, and confirm and strengthen it in that pursuit. The God that is the object of union in mystical contemplation is no other than the absolute that is sought through natural mysticism, although they approach different aspects of the divine mystery. It is also probable that natural mysticism could make an important contribution to our understanding of the mystical life, not only in terms of disciphering the various mixtures of the two kinds of contemplation that have appeared during the course of history, but also in helping us deal with the delicate transitional periods between meditation and contemplation. Is it possible, for example, that the techniques of natural mysticism could be taken up in the life of prayer and help someone to leave behind a certain kind of discursive activity that is no longer appropriate? Would these kinds of natural contemplative activities ease the pain of those people who can no longer meditate as they did before, and yet cannot be sure that they are called to go by the way of infused contemplation? Certainly, there are not going to be any easy answers to these kinds of questions, but Maritain's work on the three contemplations at least puts us in a position to ask them without having to fear that we will compromise the essential distinctions that exist among them, while his distinction between the essential and the existential encourages us to go forward and explore this terrain.

(2) Our second task is to examine more closely Maritain's intense involvement with his own times. First we will look at Maritain's involvement in the arts and how it influenced his development of the idea of the spiritual unconscious, and then we will try to place him more precisely in the metaphysical and mystical renewal that took place in Catholic circles in the first part of the century, as well as in the history of comparative religion of that period.

Jacques and Raissa always had a deep attraction to the arts and it was natural for them to apply the principles they found in St. Thomas to the creative process and the particular challenges that artists and poets face. We have already noted their friendship with Georges Rouault which helped them in their first formulation of these ideas that appeared in 1920 in **Art and Scholasticism.** This whole process would not have been possible in the same way without Raissa's own vocation as a poet, but even given this fact, which encouraged Jacques to go forward with his philosophical reflections in this area, it is still remarkable how deeply involved they were in the arts. In fact, if there have been critics that have thought that Maritain was too traditional and too aligned to the old Thomistic commentators, there have been others who have accused the Maritains of using their Thomism as an excuse to indulge their interest in the arts. Such a criticism betrays a failure to grasp how fused together in the Maritains' lives were their commitment to the essential principles of St. Thomas and to the best of artistic activity they found in their own times. It is this marriage of interests that gave rise to the range of writings that embraced the various editions of **Art and Scholasticism, The Frontiers of Poetry, The Situation of Poetry, The Responsibility of the Artist,** and **Creative Intuition in Art and Poetry.** These works were not written in the abstract, but emerged out of an ever deeper philosophical reflection and the warm friendship of many of the major artists of the times. Marc Chagal and Gino Severini, for example, both left their visual impressions of Raissa, and the Maritains were close to novelists like Henri Ghéon and Julian Greene, composers like Éric Satie, Nicolas Nabokoff and Arthur Lourie, as well as to poets like Jean Cocteau and Paul Sabon. Even

in the quieter years of Princeton when Maritain was
preparing his Mellon lectures on the fine arts he could
draw on the help of his friends like the literary critic
Francis Fergusson and the poet Allen Tate, and lest the
Maritains feel homesick for France, André Girard, a
student of Rouault, covered the walls of their home on
Linden Lane with Parisian street scenes.

In previous chapters we have been discovering how
Maritain, at decisive moments in the development of his
thought, turned to the subject and its existential depths,
and I think that it would be possible to trace a similar
evolution in regard to his ideas on art and poetry. If such
an analysis were carried out it would probably show how
Art and Scholasticism concentrated on the objective
nature of art by considering the difference between the
speculative and practical orders and art as an intellectual
virtue, but when we reach **Creative Intuition in Art and
Poetry** the emphasis is on the subjectivity of the artist
and the creative processes that take place there. Such
an analysis would have to look at Maritain's 1938 essay,
"The Experience of the Poet" as one of the major transitional points in this development. 1938, as you will
recall, was the year that saw the appearance of Maritain's essay on natural mysticism, and it was also the
time of the appearance of his essay of Freudian psychoanalysis. I would like to think that there was an inner
connection between these three events that found
expression in his ideas on the spiritual unconscious that
appeared in the various editions of his essay on the
immanent dialectic of the first act of freedom from 1945
to 1947.

"The Experience of the Poet," which had been occasioned by a series of articles by Marcel de Corte, which
appeared in the **Revue Thomiste** and elsewhere between
1936 and early 1938 on the ontology of poetry, finds
Maritain repeating his earlier themes that poetic knowledge is not aimed at knowing but making. But now he
goes on and asks himself why this is so, and looks to
subjectivity for the answer: "Subjectivity is intimately
concerned with the privileges of spirituality and of the
immanence proper to the personality itself. A subjectivity
is a spiritual subsistence and existence, which are radically active, sources of the superexistence of knowledge

and the superexistence of love." (11) Subjectivity is "a universe of productive vitality and spiritual emanation." (12)

Then Maritain goes on, in a passage that prefigures many of the themes that were to appear later in his **Creative Intuition in Art and Poetry** to write: "But if an experience of the self by the self grasps the subject **as subject**... then such an experience will be by that very fact a fecundation, as it were, of that very productivity. And such a grasp of the substance of the subject can only take place in a non-conceptual or non-logical mode, hence in an essentially obscure manner, at the very instant when some reality from the universe outside is grasped by the mode of affective connaturality, in an intuitive emotion in which the universe and the subject are revealed together to the subject, as if by a beam of darkness." (13)

And much to our point he characterizes this poetic knowledge as "unconscious" and later as "hidden in the spiritual unconscious." (14) This poetic knowledge is one of several "experiences of existence" which include "the Hindu contemplation of the Self." (15) The soul of the poet remains "available to itself." It "keeps as it were a reserve of spirituality" which is "like a sleep of the soul; being **of the spirit**... it is itself in act, I say virtually, by way of a tension and a virtual reversion of the spirit on itself and on all that is in it. The soul sleeps but its heart is awake, let it sleep... " (16)

These lines are the forerunners of Maritain's later remarks on Fr. Osende's unconscious prayer of the heart, and this whole essay as a culmination of his ideas on the creative process becomes one of the foundations for his development of the theme of the spiritual unconscious.

Another source for this same development is be found in Maritain's only essay devoted entirely to Freudian psychoanalysis. During the Meudon years Maritain would listen to his friend Roland Dalbiez read passages from what was to become Dalbiez's extensive **La méthode psychoanalytique et la doctrine freudienne**, which appeared in 1936. Despite Maritain's reservations about Freudian philosophy which he feels has marred Freud's psychology, he considers Freud's "technique for the exploration of the geological depths of the soul" to be "a discovery of the

highest importance." (17) And once Maritain became
conversant with Freud's work, how could he fail to be
struck by the fact that the idea of the unconscious is
latent in St. Thomas' view of the soul:

"For St. Thomas Aquinas, not only is the human soul
obscure to itself, - knowing its own concrete existence
only by reflection on its acts, - not only are its basic
tendencies, called powers or faculties, among the realities whose intimate nature escapes introspection, but, in
addition, the instincts, the inclinations, the acquired
tendencies, the **habitus** or internal improvements of the
faculties, the virtues and the vices, the deep mechanisms
of the life of the spirit - all these constitute a world of
reality **whose effects alone reach consciousness.**" (18)

Once this insight has sprung forth, then he has a
vantage point from which to criticize Freud's work:
"Freud invented a powerful instrument for exploring the
unconscious, and beheld with deepest insight this fearful
world, the interior inferno, full of all the monsters
repressed in the unconscious. But he mixed up the unconscious itself with this inferno, which is only part of it.
He separated it from the life of reason and of the
spirit." (19) When we read these two passages we see
that it would be only another step to distinguish the
Freudian unconscious from the spiritual unconscious
already implied in Christain metaphysical and mystical
traditions, but not yet brought to conscious realization.

This essay, therefore, becomes the second pillar after
"The Experience of the Poet" in the development of the
idea of the spiritual unconscious. The third and fourth can
be found in his essay on natural mysticism and his
thoughts on mystical contemplation which we have already
examined, and a fifth, largely undeveloped, in his reflections on the intuition of being. Previously we had traced
the genesis of Maritain's spiritual unconscious to his essay
on the immanent dialectic, and now we can see its roots
are in the works of 1938 which sum up long researches
in these different areas, and which in this year flow
closer together to form the matrix from which the idea
of the spiritual unconscious will later be born.

The pattern of involvement of Maritain in the arts
that we have just briefly reviewed exists, as well, in his
metaphysical and mystical work which can be situated in

relationship to the Thomistic rediscovery of esse, the
renewal of mystical theology, and the development of a
Catholic comparative mysticism.

Maritain's philosophical thought, though it owed most
to his reading of St. Thomas and his commentators,
profited from his relationship to three Dominican priests,
Humbert Clérissac, Père Dehau and Reginald Garrigou-
Lagrange who have already made their appearance in the
previous chapters. Père Clérissac was their first spiritual
director and introduced Raissa to the **Summa**. Jacques
used to go off in the morning and serve his Mass and
then have long conversations on philosophical and theological matters, and it was Fr. Clérissac who helped him
prepare his first philosophical article in 1910. Of Père
Dehau, their second director, Jacques writes in his
Notebooks: "As for me, I passed hours - priceless hours
- reading John of St. Thomas to Father Dehau, and
listening to his commentaries. What keys he gave me,
what enlightenments I received from his brilliant intelligence! (It went more quickly with the affairs of my
'interior,' which moreover did not offer much that was
remarkable. Is not a philosopher, moreover, intended for
the common good of the republic of minds? Sometimes
I bore a little grudge against this common good.) (20) And
before the war it was to Garrigou-Lagrange that they
turned, together with Charles Henrion, to pose questions
about the mystical life. It was to Garrigou-Lagrange,
long-time professor at the Angelicum in Rome, that they
went in 1918, when they came to Rome for the first
time, bearing Jacques' massive manuscript on the appari-
tions of Our Lady at La Salette, and it was to him they
looked when they sought a spiritual director for the
Thomist circle and its retreats. Jacques called his theological teaching "a light of grace and a blessing for our
intelligence." (21)

In 1922 Maritain met Yves Simon who was one of his
students at the Institut Catholique, and went on to
become Maritain's life-long friend and a distinguished
philosopher in his own right. Their extensive correspondence is being prepared for publication. In 1923, Etienne
Gilson sent Maritain a revised edition of his **Le
Thomisme,** a gesture that began their long friendship. It
is interesting to note in connection with the role that

this book was to play in the rediscovery of esse that
even at this early date Maritain made a number of
suggestions that Gilson took advantage of in later editions. In a 1924 letter Maritain touched on the theme of
the essential and the existential when he wrote to Gilson:
"The man to whom St. Thomas addresses his moral doctrine is not Aristotle's man; it is not human nature in
the abstract state, but human nature taken in its fallen
and concrete redeemed condition." (22) Their friendship
gradually deepened and took a decisive turn at a meeting
at the home of the Russian philosopher Berdiaeff in
January, 1931, where Jacques spoke on St. Thomas and
philosophy in the faith at a time when the debate on
Christian philosophy was growing. "Berdiaeff turns towards
Gilson, counting on him to contradict me and reminding
him what he wrote in his book on Thomism apropos of
St. Thomas as a precursor of the philosophy of pure
reason. To the great surprise of all, Gilson declares that
if he spoke thus he erred, and that he is entirely in
agreement with me. (He, in fact, considerably changed
his positions in the later editions of Le Thomisme.) Raissa
and I are very touched by the attitude of Gilson and by
his honesty in correcting himself. From this day dates our
ties of friendship with him." (23) A little while later
Gilson was instrumental in inviting Maritain to lecture
for the first time in North America at the Institute of
Medieval Studies in Toronto. These particular episodes are
just symbolic of Maritain's philosophical and theological
style, and as the publication of his enormous correspondence proceeds this picture of deep reflection joined to
personal relationships will become clearer.

Maritain also took part in the tremendous revival of
Catholic mystical theology during the first decades of
this century. Mystical theology, battered by the crisis of
Quietism at the end of the 17th century, had fallen
silent, and grown isolated from theology. At the turn of
the century, Abbé Saudreau had begun to breathe life
back into it with works like **Les degrées de la vie
spirituelle** in 1896 and **L'etat mystique** in 1903. He soon
came into conflict with Auguste Poulain whose **Les grâces
d'oraison** had appeared in 1901. They differed over the
existence of an acquired contemplation in the writings
of the Carmelite saints, a controversy that had disturbed

the 17th century as well, and allied with this problem were differing conceptions of the mystical life and thus the call to it. The following years saw an outpouring of books and articles on these themes, as well as the whole of the spiritual life. There was Père Louis de Besse's, **La science de la prière,** Dom Vital Lehodey's, **Les voies de l'oraison mentale** (1908), and Père Laballe's **La contemplation** (1912). Later came Bremond's, **Histoire littéraire de sentiment religieux en France** (1916-1922), and work of men like Juan Arintero and Garrigou-Lagrange whose **Perfection chrétienne et contemplation** appeared in 1923, and many others.

One of the major currents of this renewal was a fresh look at the work of John of the Cross by Carmelite authors like Crisógono de Jesús, Claudio de Jesús Crucificado, and Gabriel de Sainte Marie-Magdeleine. In 1926 St. John was declared a doctor of the Church, and in 1929-31 Silverio de Santa Teresa published the first critical edition of his works. 1920 saw the publication of **La vie spirituelle** under the direction of M.V. Bernadot and **La revue d'ascétique et de mystique** edited by J. de Guibert.

Maritain was very much a part of this world. He read the classic works like John of St. Thomas on the gifts of the Holy Spirit, and the Carmelite Joseph of the Holy Spirit, and he admired the modern classics as well: Fr. Gardeil's, **La structure de l'ame,** and Garrigou-Lagrange's, **Christian Perfection and Contemplation** and **The Love of God and Cross of Jesus.** His own 1923 letter to **La vie spirituelle** echoes the debates raging at the time, as well as his relationship with Fr. Lagrange. He regretted the interpretation that Jean Baruzi gave to John of the Cross and wrote a preface to his friend Bruno de Jesus-Marie's life of the mystical doctor. In short, he drank in the best of this mystical revival and made a major contribution to it himself.

And it was his mastery of the Catholic metaphysical and mystical traditions that allowed him to contribute to a third current of these times, the birth of a Catholic comparative mysticism. Henri de Lubac, in his preface to a later milestone in this field, **La mystique et les mystiques,** suggests that the revival of Catholic mystical studies that we have just seen was to join the study of

comparative religions to give birth to a distinctive
Catholic comparative mysticism. (23a)

The Catholic study of comparative religions had taken
a new turn in 1911 and 1912 with the publication of two
collaborative efforts: **Où en est l'histoire des religions**
editied by Abbé Bricout, and **Christus, manuel d'historie
des religions** directed by Joseph Huby. These developments had had their forerunners in traditional Catholic
theology with the debates on implicit and explicit faith,
and the salvation of unbelievers that we saw Maritain
refer to in his essay on the immanent dialectic.

The whole project of a Catholic comparative mysticism received a boost later from Joseph Marechal's
Studies in the Psychology of the Mystics, and began to
find more definitive expression when philosophers and
theologians were joined by Catholic specialists in other
mystical traditions. In the front ranks of these scholars
was Louis Massingnon who wrote his thesis at the Sorbonne on the Islamic mystic Al Hâllaj. Jacques and
Charles Henrion had met him before the war, and
Jacques had kept in touch with him over the years;
Charles de Foucauld, who undoubtedly influenced this
whole movement by his life among the Tuareg in North
Africa, was another link among these three men. When
Jacques wrote his chapter VI in **The Degrees of Know-
ledge** on mystical experience and philosophy he cites
Massingnon at the head of a list of authors that included
Miguel Asin Palacios, Martin Buber, W. Schmidt, W.
Wallace on Hindu spirituality and Olivier Lacombe's,
"Orient et Occident" which appeared in the **Etudes
Carmélitaines** in April 1931. Massingnon was to influence
George Anawati and Louis Gardet, and we have already
seen how Maritain's philosophical reflections were to join
with the expertise of Lacombe and Gardet to give rise
to a distinctive theory of comparative mysticism.

This work helped to fulfill part of the promise of the
future that Maritain had foreseen in his preface to
Dandoy's, **The Ontology of the Vedanta:** "We are only at
the first beginnings of a work of which Louis Massingnon,
with his great book on Al Hâllaj, has been one of the
pioneers in France. The work pursued in Calcutta by Fr.
Dandoy and his collaborators at **The Light of the East,**
whose French translation on the study of the Advaita is

being published today, gives us the hope that it will be fruitful, and the hard labor begun 300 years ago by Fr. de Nobili will succeed in having an important philosophical and theological harvest in the 20th century." (24)

This work in India was, in fact, to be continued later by men like Jules Monchanin and Henri le Saux, and until his recent death was carried on by Bede Griffiths at his Hindu-Christian ashram, Shantivanam. A similar process has taken place in Japan through Hugo Lasalle and the other Catholic students of the Zen master Koun Yamada who have become recognized Zen teachers in their own right. While it does not appear that Maritain's work on natural mysticism had much influence on these later developments in India and Japan, he did have an important effect on his friend Thomas Merton who went on to be a major participant in the east-west dialogue, and we can only hope that the Maritain-Lacombe-Gardet current of natural mysticism will go on and enrich the efforts of today's participants in the Church's encounter with Hinduism and Buddhism.

(3) Maritain thought of himself as a philosopher, and it would be possible to refine our brief portrait of his place in his times by situating him in the 20th century history of Thomism. Then he would find his place between the Thomism of his two friends Fr. Lagrange and Etienne Gilson, and this whole current of the Thomistic renaissance could be contrasted, in turn, with the transcendental Thomism springing from the work of Rousselot and Maréchal. But this is a task that has been carried out in a number of different ways (25), and I think it will be more revealing to look at Maritain within a larger framework, for then we might get a glimpse of how the future might see him, as one of Thomism's greatest figures. And then we can ask, as well, just what qualities contributed to this greatness.

The idea of Christian philosophy was no abstraction for Maritain; it was a natural state of being, as it were. We have seen how he did not find his definitive philosophical path until after his conversion and his early spiritual formation, and once he found this road he saw that philosophy, theology and a fervent life of prayer, far from being antagonistic to each other, were meant to dwell together harmoniously.

This road as a Christian philospher, especially as a Thomist Christian philosopher, however congenial it was to be for him personally, was not to be an easy one. He tells the story of an old lady, whom he venerated, who told his friends: "He is a Catholic, you know, but of a peculiar sect. He is also a Thomist." (26) At a more serious level, the idea of being a believing Christian and a genuine philosopher met incomprehension among the secular philosophers of France, an incomprehension Maritain understood well, but suffered from nonetheless. No matter how much the Christian philosopher may strive to do philosophy: "Even so he will scarcely manage to avoid misunderstanding. Even if he went to the length of asking pardon for being a Christian and of assuming an air of detachment and of dehumanisation and of passing for a thinker in the state of pure nature, who leaves his soul with his cloak at the university cloakroom, even though he dried up deliberately the sources of his intellectual vitality, he will not put them on the wrong scent; he will never manage to reassure people about himself entirely." (27)

The problem is even more acute when the subject is moral philosophy, which receives its object from theology, for he is "suspected by the theologians because he is a philosopher, and by the philosophers because his philosophy takes into account the things of faith." (28) He concludes in an autobiographical vein: "Is it surprising therefore that the Christian philosopher is in an uncomfortable position? He believes in a supernatural order, and as life will not permit this to be 'put into parentheses' he suffers for it." (29)

Gilson, with a fondness for a good story, recounts in his **The Philosopher and Theology** that Maritain was virtually ignored in certain French philosophical circles, and when he spoke "his usual language" at a meeting of the French Society of Philosophy in 1936: "A philsopher who had come from Mars for the occasion would not have been less understood. The excellent Bouglé was the least fanatic among the representatives of secular philosophy. He was most anxious that his Catholic colleagues should feel they were trusted by him, and as a result he strove to prove it to them by courageous decisions. He came

out of this meeting visibly preoccupied, even worried.
'Say,' he whispered in my ear, taking me by the arm in
a friendly way, 'what is the matter with him? I think he
is crazy!" (30)

It was this kind of incomprehension on the part of
some of his countrymen who regarded his work as non-
existant (31), that probably played a significant role in
his decision, after his ambassadorship in Rome, to go to
the United States to pursue his philosophical career. Here
he was well received in both Catholic and non-Catholic
circles, but he was not entirely freed from the same kind
of misunderstanding. On the ocassion of receiving an
invitation to speak at a university he remarked to his
secretary Cornelia Borgerhoff: "You notice that it was
the department of religion that asked me, not the
department of philosophy." (32)

This is but one of a series of problems and paradoxes
that surrounded Maritain's philosophical work which were
masterfully summed up by the author of the unsigned
présentation to the Maritain volume of the **Revue
Thomiste**. There is a striking contrast between "the most
energetic and violently new thought, penetrated by passion
and poetry, and the most technical armature... new
thought, but springing from that of St. Thomas and even
the school of St. Thomas... applied to the solution of the
typical problems of our era and, even more, deepened and
bettered according to its proper genius." (33)

Maritain "enters into the interior itself of that thought
from which the profane current of philosophy had with-
drawn three centuries ago, and which the theologians
alone, when they do not fear isolation, continue to
exploit for the solution of their proper problems... He
pursues its progress which seems to have stopped with
John of St. Thomas." (34) And the price he pays is that:
"In university circles Maritain remains for many the
scholastic, the Thomist..." while among Catholics he looks
"too little conciliating, too abrupt, too Thomist, or, at
least, too much a friend of the commentators. And why
not say it. Too difficult... not at all the popularizer."
(35)

But these paradoxes resolve themselves once we see
them in the proper perspective. As we saw in chapter I,
Maritain did not embrace a ready-made Thomism as a

convenient philosophical appendix to his Catholic faith. It was certainly crucial that his philosophy be in harmony with his faith, as his struggles in Heidelberg over Bergson's ideas on the concept showed. But it was also vital that this philosophy meet his deepest philosophical aspirations and questions, questions he was struggling with when he was a Bergsonian. With Thomas he found a way to articulate his earlier insights like that of the intuition of being which had sprung up through the concrete approach of Bergson's duration, and while becoming a Thomist had the appearance of isolating him from the world he had grown up in, it was, in fact, a great liberation.

Maritain was a Thomist because he penetrated its living reality and substance, so that it was no longer Thomas' philosophy or John of St. Thomas', but his own. For it was only if it was his own that he could apply it with such vigor and creativity to contemporary problems. There is a great difference between looking at a philosophy from the outside and seeing it from within. The first way can lead to a certain amount of erudition, but often becomes philosphy talking about philosophy. The second way means assimilating the very marrow of this philosophy and becoming a living part of a philosophical tradition, which in the case of Thomism stretches back through the commentators to St. Thomas and further to Albert the Great and Augustine, and to the early Greeks and the Scriptures. Maritain is not someone simply trying to understand the great Thomists at a distance and make them the foils of an intellectual exercise that has as its unspoken goal a demonstration of their limitations and his own superior insight, but rather he entered into intimate conversation with them about the living mystery of being that they all served by their work. This is quite different than either a scholasticism in which the technical apparatus and the words themselves have become a dead weight, or a contemporary philosophy alive with creative intuition, but constrained to reinvent the whole of philosophy on the ruins of previous systems.

It is worthwhile to explore further the relationship Maritain has with Thomas and his commentators or continuers, as he would have preferred to call them. In a preface to John of St. Thomas' material logic Maritain comments: "Philosophy lives on dialogue and conversation and it is a mark of any great philosophy that it can manifest constantly new aspects in a conversation pursued through centuries on the same accepted principles and with organic consistency. A philosopher finds reason for melancholy in realizing that the conversation about his own ideas (assuming that he is worthy of it) will begin only when he is dead and no longer has the opportunity of having his search for truth profit from it. Fortunate is he, if the very meaning of his deepest intuitions is not missed by the interlocutors. To continue the conversation with congenial and clearsighted companions of Cajetan, Bañez and John of St. Thomas is a privilege of the genius of Thomas Aquinas and of his grace-given mission." (36)

The melancholy in this passage is Maritain's own, and we will return to it later. But these words also allow us to glimpse something of the interior dialogues that Maritain kept up for so many years with the great Thomists. Maritain's deep and prolonged meditation on the classic Thomistic texts can be seen in a striking way in **The Degrees of Knowledge**. In appendix IV, for example, on the notion of subsistence he makes reference to Thomas' **Summa Theologiae, De Potentia, De Veritate, De Spiritualibus Creaturis, Summa Contra Gentiles** and so forth, and goes on to Cajetan's **In de Ente et Essentia**, and contemporary debates. In appendix I, which deals with the concept, he cites the logic and **Cursus Theologicus** of John of St. Thomas and an even wider array of St. Thomas' writings than in appendix IV. And this intensive reading of the past is not done with a primarily historical intent, but to discover the deepest root principles, and bring them to bear on vital contemporary issues.

It is in his relationship with John of St. Thomas that we can catch a glimpse of how he must have seen the ultimate import of his own work, although he was too modest to state it explicitly. For Maritain, John of St. Thomas (1589-1644) was "the guide par excellence in the exploration of the great depths of the **perennial philosophy**," (37) and Maritain wondered what would have happened if the world had followed John of St. Thomas rather than his contemporary Descartes. It was the vocation of John of St. Thomas to be "the last great repre-

sentative of the traditions of the schools, the metaphysical and theological heritage assembled by Greek and
Christian wisdom." (38) And Maritain could appreciate the
irony of this carrier of wisdom of the past being on the
margin of contemporary thought which could not see what
he had to offer, while he, himself, hid this wisdom under
the cover of a scholastic methodology that made it
unassimilable by his time. "He separated metaphysics
from the age and confined it in the heaven of theology."
(39) The result was that he "put in reserve the most
elevated goods of the philosophical and theological tradition for a future time that would know how to extract
them from their scholastic matrix (gangue scolaire)." (40)

If we translate this into more personal terms, Maritain
saw that he could be one of the people who received this
treasure, and refined the precious ore that was imbedded
in John of St. Thomas' interminable scholastic debates.
We have already seen how Maritain felt isolated by being
a Christian philsopher in an age that could no longer
understand such a thing, but he was not going to follow
John of St. Thomas' footsteps in withdrawing from the
marketplace. When Maritain writes that there is to be
found in John of St. Thomas "a powerful poetic élan, a
sovereign force of intuition, an acuteness of gaze of
transcendent simplicity" he really could be describing
himself, just as he inadvertently did in "Reflexions sur la
nature blessée" when he spoke of "la hardiesse du
regard." And when in regard to John of St. Thomas'
treatise of the gifts of the Holy Spirit he sees prolonged
in a new synthesis "the thought of St. Thomas, enlarging
the frontiers of Thomism with a daring all the more
great because it was founded on the powerful and vehe-
ment adhesion to the spirit and organic principles of
Thomism," we have an exact description of what he,
himself, attempted to do.

"Jacques had no taste for the past," wrote his niece
Eveline Gardiner. "It was the future that was important
to him." (41) And Jacques said of himself: "What am I,
I asked myself then. A professor? I think not; I taught
by necessity. A writer? Perhaps. A philosopher? I hope
so. But also a kind of romantic of justice too prompt to
imagine himself, at each combat entered into, that justice
and truth will have their day among men. And also

perhaps a kind of spring-finder who presses his ear to the
ground in order to hear the sound of hidden springs, and
of invisible germinations." (42)

By means of his keen intuition, Maritain never stopped
listening for the sounds of these hidden springs. In the
last summers of his life, he would leave Toulouse and
stay with his friends the Gruneliuses in Kolbsheim near
Strasbourg. But there he always devoted himself to his
philosophical work, not in the sense of finding answers
that could be mechanically passed on, but "to scout the
trails, to open the roads for those who would continue
the work of searching for the truth which he held so
much to heart." (43) It was this search for truth that he
considered his vocation and his way to serve, as he
commented in his **Notebooks,** "the common good of the
republic of minds." In contrast to his philosophical work,
in the same passage he makes an allusion to his own
interior life: "It went more quickly with the affairs of
my 'interior,' which moreover did not offer much that
was remarkable." Even these notebooks do not dispel the
reserve that Maritain had about speaking of his own spiritual life. He saw his **Notebooks** as setting the stage for
Raissa's journals. But there is no doubt about his dedication to the life of prayer. He would go to Mass every
day, and on his visits to the University of Notre Dame,
"people were astounded at the many hours that he spent
kneeling before the Blessed Sacrament." (44)

On one occasion he let this veil of silence slip.
Wallace Fowlie, a friend of Maritain and a professor of
French literature was visiting him and told him how he
had been a student of T.S. Eliot at Harvard, and served
Mass at the Anglican chapel where Eliot was a daily
communicant. One day when he was serving Mass with
Eliot as the only participant, he heard a thud and turned
to see Eliot stretched out on the floor in the grips,
apparently, of some sort of religious experience. "At the
end of the story, tears were rolling down Jacques's
cheeks. He recovered quickly, smiled at me, and said: "I
am going to tell you a story about myself, a comparable
story... The first year that President Hutchins invited me
to give a course at the University of Chicago, I made
arrangements to attend the earliest mass each morning
at the Cathedral of the Holy Name. One morning after

I received communion, I must have had the same experience, the same need that Eliot had and that you described. I stretched out, face down, at the altar rail. There were only a few people, and they had gone back to their seats. It was dark in the church. A janitor came by and kicked me in the side, saying, 'We don't allow drunks in this church.' He forced me to get up." (45)

The reader of Raissa's journals cannot fail to notice the great deal of suffering that she underwent, and Jacques shared in those trials. Despite all the signs of outward success that his work received, he suffered from a melancholy that seemed to grow deeper as he grew older, especially when Raissa was no longer at his side. He turned to his friends like Julian Greene and Thomas Merton and wrote them of his misgivings and trials. Where others saw creativity and genius, he saw defects and limitations.

"And my own solitude? It seems to me that it was that of a kind of clumsy diver, advancing as best he could in the midst of the submarine fauna of captive truths and of the larvae of the time. One will never know to what temptations of black sadness and despair a philosopher can be exposed in proportion as he descends into the knowledge of himself and of the great pity which is in the world. His rest here on earth will finally be in the night, if in this night, which is nearer to God than the day, and more desolate too, an invisible hand which he loves leads him like a blind man." (46)

One of the secrets of Maritain's greatness resides in the fact that he was truly a Christian philosopher. His metaphysics was nourished by a soul given to prayer, and his philosophy put at the service of theology and mysticism. His doctrine of the three contemplations marks him not only as a great metaphysician, but as a pioneering spiritual writer who has opened the way to a deeper understanding of the mysticism of the self and supernatural contemplation.

NOTES

(1) "Pas de savoir sans intuitivité" in **Approches sans entraves,** p. 412.

(2) An Essay in **Christian Philosophy,** New York, Philosophical Library, 1955, p. 11. Translated from **De la philosophie chrétienne,** Paris, Desclée de Brouwer, 1933.

(3) **Ibid.,** p. 30.

(4) **Ibid.,** p. 39.

(5) Approches sans entraves, p. 254.

(6) **Ibid.,** p. 258.

(7) **Ibid.,** p. 261.

(8) **Science and Wisdom,** New York, Scribner's Sons, 1940, p. 25. Translated from **Science et Sagesse,** Paris, La Bergerie, 1935.

(9) **Ibid.,** p. 87-88.

(10) **Ibid.,** p. 86-87, note 1.

(11) "The Experience of the Poet" in **The Situation of Poetry,** New York, Philosophical Library, 1955, p. 72. Translated from **Situation de la poésie,** Paris, Desclée de Brouwer, 1938.

(12) **Ibid.,** p. 73.

(13) **Ibid.**

(14) **Ibid.,** p. 80.

(15) **Ibid.,** p. 74.

(16) **Ibid.,** p. 81.

(17) "Freudianism and Psychoanalysis" in **Scholasticism and Politics,** Garden City, New York, Image Books, 1960, p. 145.

(18) **Ibid.,** p. 141.

(19) **Ibid.,** p. 157.

(20) Notebooks, p. 79.

(21) **Ibid.**

(22) Cited in Laurence Shook, "Maritain and Gilson: Early Relations" in **Thomistic Papers II,** edited by L.A. Kennedy and J.C. Marler, Houston, Center for Thomistic Studies, 1986, p. 20.

(23) Notebooks, p. 163.

(23a) La mystique et les mystiques, directed by A. Ravier, Desclée de Brouwer, 1965. See also Thomas O'Meara, "Exploring the Depths. A Theological Tradition in Viewing the World Religions" in the Fries Festschrift. For Garrigou-Lagrange's outlook: "Prémystique naturelle et mystique surnaturelle" in Etudes Carmélitaines, 2, (1933), p. 51-77.

(24) "Commentaire au livre de G. Dandoy, L'Ontologie de Vedânta" in Oeuvres Complètes, Vol. IV, p. 1058.

(25) Cf. Helen John, The Thomist Spectrum, New York, Fordham University Press, 1966, and Gerald McCool, From Unity to Pluralism, New York, Fordham University Press, 1988.

(26) Jacques Maritain. Son oeuvre philosophique, Paris, Bibliothèque de la Revue Thomiste, 1948, p. xi.

(27) Science and Wisdom, p. 94.

(28) Ibid.

(29) Ibid.

(30) Etienne Gilson, The Philosopher and Theology, New York, Random House, 1962, p. 203.

(31) Cahiers Jacques Maritain, 4-5, p. 10-11.

(32) Interview.

(33) Jacques Maritain. Son oeuvre philosophique, p. v.

(34) Ibid.

(35) Ibid., p. vi.

(36) Oeuvres Complètes, Vol.   , p. 1174.

(37) Oeuvres Complètes, Vol.   , p. 1017.

(38) Ibid., p. 1022.

(39) Ibid., p. 1023.

(40) Ibid., p. 1024.

(40a) Ibid., p. 1026-1027.

(41) "Souvenir sur mon oncle" in Cahiers Jacques Maritain, 2, p. 16.

(42) Notebooks, p. 3.

(43) Antoinette Grunelius, "Jacques Maritain et Kolbsheim" in Cahiers Jacques Maritain, 4-5, p. 95.

(44) Leo R. Ward, "Meeting Jacques Maritain" in The Review of Politics, Vol. 44, October, 1982, no. 4, p. 485.

(45) Wallace Fowlie, "Remembering Jacques Maritain" in The American Scholar.

(46) Notebooks, p. 74.

(47) A careful examination of these events can be found in Bernard Doering, Jacques Maritain and the French Catholic Intellectuals. Notre Dame, IN: Univ. of Notre Dame Press, 1983.

CHAPTER V

THE SPIRITUAL UNCONSCIOUS

Our detailed examination of Maritain's thoughts on the three contemplations has led us to an unexpected discovery of great significance. The deeper we probed, the more we saw how seemingly disparate strands of Maritain's work converged towards the idea of the spiritual unconscious. It is out of the rich and mysterious depths of this unconscious that the intuition of being, mystical contemplation, and the mysticism of the self all emerge, each in its distinctive way.

But it is clear that if Maritain's pioneering efforts have opened up the door to this interior universe, it still remains to be seen whether we will have the initiative and energy to enter in and explore it. If previously we searched for the origins of this idea in Maritain's thought, now we have to take a closer look at the state of development it reached in his final works, that is, in **The Peasant of the Garonne, On the Grace and Humanity of Jesus,** and **Approches sans entraves.** Once we have done this, we will be in a position to see what paths the idea of the spiritual unconscious opens up for the future.

In Maritain's 1966 **The Peasant of the Garonne** we find not only the incidental use of phrases like, "the heaven of the soul" (1) or "be it in the unconscious" (2), but several occasions where the idea of the spiritual unconscious is strongly developed.

The intellect, for example, "is helped and prodded, in order to work well much more often than philosophers and scientists are willing to admit, by "intuition," or flashes of the imagination - they come to it unexpectedly, with the luck of the road, from the vigilance of sense and poetic instinct, or are born in the night of the unconscious (let us say rather, of the preconscious or supra-conscious of the spirit)." (3)

This kind of intuition, connected with the imagination, is not yet the intuition of being, which is an "intellectual intuition" which comes to "whoever manages to enter into that alert and watchful silence of the mind where, consenting to the **simplicity** of the true, the intellect becomes sufficiently available, and vacant, and open, to hear what all things murmur, and to **listen,** instead of fashioning answers. Many have actually had this intuition who were too distracted by everyday life or their own reasonings to become aware of it. And many more among the common people experience it in this way than among "cultured" people. And it is enough to look at the gaze of certain children to realize that, without their having in them any of the reflectiveness of adults, their gaze is directed more at **being** than at the toys with which one amuses them, or even at the world whose riches they constantly discover simply by taking the trouble to receive them." (4)

It is important to grasp the import of this passage. The intellect must become available, vacant and open to depths that go beyond the normal conceptual working of the mind, which Maritain calls fashioning answers. If this were not true, there would be no way to understand how the central insights of Thomism could be obscure to so many people who have been subjected to it in countless classrooms. Maritain will continue this passage by saying, "I will not try and describe what escapes any restraint and is beyond any word... nor to lead someone where access is given only in pure solitude of soul." (5) Then he goes on to cite the now familiar passages from **A Preface to Metaphysics** - "it is nothing for me to crush a fly" - and Raissa's "a powerful intuition whose violence sometimes frightened me."

It is easy to see that Maritain is one small step from locating the site of this intuition of being in the spiritual unconscious, and two steps away from dealing with the issue that he here turns away from when he says, "nor to lead someone where access is given only in purest solitude of soul."

The step, in regards to the spiritual unconscious, comes in the next chapter in a passage I have already cited without comment in Chapter I. It is a place of such importance that it demands to be cited in its entirety:

"There is nothing simpler than to think **I am, I exist**, this blade of grass exists; this gesture of the hand, this captivating smile that the next instant will hurry away, **exist**; the world **exists**. The all-important thing is for such a perception to sink deeply enough within me that my awareness of it will strike me some day sharply enough (at times, violently) to stir and move my intellect up to that very world of preconscious activity, beyond any word or formula, and with no assignable boundaries, which nourishes everything within it. Such a descent to the very depths of the soul is doubtless something **given**, not **worked out** - given by the natural grace of the intellectual nature.

And then, if luck should take a hand, and if the eye of consciousness, sufficiently accustomed to the half-light, should penetrate a little, like a thief, this limbo of the preconscious, it can come about that this simple **I am** will seem like a revelation in the night - a secret revelation which will awaken echoes and surprises on all sides and give a hint of the inexhaustible ampleness it permits one to attain.

And there can be instances, as I noted in the foregoing chapter, where this experience is genuinely present in someone who takes no notice of it, either because it remains involved in the more or less superficial layers of consciousness, or because, as with children, it takes place only the preconscious of the spirit.

It is in a judgment (or in a preconscious act equivalent to an unformulated judgment), and in a judgment of existence, that the intellectual intuition of being occurs. The philosophical concept of the **actus essendi**, of the act of existence, will only come later." (6)

Maritain has recalled his remarks in the previous chapter and pushed them to their logical conclusion. The intuition of being takes place in "that very world of preconscious activity," "the depths of the soul," "this limbo of the preconscious." All this is the ultimate corrective to the faults of "notionalism and a fixation upon abstract essences" (7) which, again and again, have reared their heads during the course of the history of Thomism. If the experience of the intuition of being takes place in the spiritual unconscious, then this will have revolutionary consequences for the whole future of

Thomistic metaphysics where it will be a question of whether it is possible "to lead someone where access is given only in purest solitude of soul." This is the first of the themes that make up the future of Maritain's thought, which we will have to pursue later in the chapter.

The other principal place in **The Peasant of the Garonne** where Maritain talks about the spiritual unconscious we have already looked at in some detail. It is the question of praying always that Maritain addresses in the context of living a life of mystical contemplation "in the very midst of the world."

"The prayer that Father Osende calls the prayer of the heart and that he describes as unconscious (it pertains to that "supra-conscious of the spirit" of which I have said a great deal elsewhere) can and must, he says, be continuous in the contemplative soul. "For we cannot fix our mind on two objects at the same time nor continue to think always, whereas we can love always" (at least in the supra-conscious of the spirit - only there, in effect, can love be **in act** continuously). We are then no longer dealing simply with the vital impulse of prayer always present **virtually** in consciousness; the prayer of the heart itself remains in act - in the supra-conscious of the spirit." (8)

As you will remember, it was here that Maritain accused himself of a "serious error" for previously imagining that such a prayer should be equated with his masked contemplation when, in fact, it is a "typical **form** of contemplation, and one of the most precious." (9) He finds the antecedents of this idea beginning very early in the history of spirituality with St. Anthony the Hermit's "there is no perfect prayer if the religious is, himself, aware that he is praying." This is a remark reported by Cassian, and thus introduced quite early in the development of Western monasticism.

What we are faced with is Maritain definitively placing the site of mystical contemplation in the spiritual unconscious. If such a perspective were taken seriously, it would provide a new perspective from which to try to deal with some of the most difficult and intractable problems in the contemplative life. If all of us are called to contemplation in the remote sense, and the more immediate call coincides with John of the Cross' three signs, and a transition to being **habitually** aided by the gifts of the Holy Spirit," and if this transition can take place, according to Maritain, "in a manner inaccessible to consciousness (in the depths of the supra-conscious of the spirit,)" (10) then we have a new way to examine questions about our conscious awareness and perception of the contemplative experience.

Again within the context of contemplation on the roads of the world, Maritain sees that mystical contemplation in its open form can be experienced in such a way that "the great signs that St. John of the Cross and St. Teresa of Avila have described do not appear..." (11) This kind of contemplation he identifies with St. Therese of Lisieux's little way "where all the great things described by St. John of the Cross can be found divinely simplified and reduced to the pure essentials..." (12)

"The soul is laid bare, and its very love-prayer as well - so arid at times that it seems to fly into distractions and emptiness." (13) This contemplation is sometimes given to those in the world in such a way that "this treasure is hidden from the souls themselves that possess it." (14) This kind of prayer can be pursued "in relationship with men" and in this dimension, as well, it can take place in the "spiritual preconscious more than the conscious..." (15) But in this case "it is an arid love-prayer, almost too pure for our feeble heart, because, being much more unconscious than conscious, it comes about in the tiredness of our members and of our conscious faculties, rather than in the repose where we can taste 'how sweet the Lord is.'" (16)

Maritain's **De la grâce et de l'humanité de Jésus** appeared in 1967 after **The Peasant of the Garonne,** but "as regards the essential point" (17) it had been written before it. This little book is a remarkable achievement in Christology, and one of the reasons that motivated Maritain to undertake this difficult task of formulating a research hypothesis on the soul of Jesus was "the central importance of the humanity of Jesus in contemplation and the contemplative life." (18) As he did in the case of **Creative Intuition in Art and Poetry,** he again took the idea of the psychological unconscious and used it as an inspiration to fashion a philosophical instrument

in terms of the spiritual unconscious, which could be
applied to some of the intractable problems in theology
about the humanity of Jesus. Both the infraconscious, as
well as in the preconscious or supra-conscious of the
spirit, "there are many dwelling-places, in other words
spheres typically different indeed, and which have
sometimes between them only a purely analogical
community." (19) And even the supra-conscious in the
sense of the natural depths of the human spirit must be
clearly distinguished from the divinized supra-consciousness of Christ, which is a "transcendent consciousness of
self." (20) This divinized supra-consciousness in Christ is
the dimension of His soul divinized by the Beatific
Vision. Another way of putting it is to say that in Christ
we can distinguish a "world of consciousness" (21) that
embraces normal self-awareness and the natural infra and
supra-consciousness from this divinized supra-consciousness
caused by the Beatific Vision and "absolutely proper to
the soul of Christ alone." (22) This divinized supra-conscious, unlike our own natural supra-conscious, was a
consciousness of self in which Jesus knew Himself in
perfect clarity as the Word of God.

This leads Maritain to distinguish in Jesus' human
nature two different states. In the soul of Jesus there
is a comprehensor state in which He enjoys this divinized
supra-conscious, but there is also a viator, or wayfarer
state in which He had a human consciousness that grew
and developed like our own. And what of the relationship
between the two states? Jesus' lower consciousness was,
in some sense, "unconscious" (23) of his higher consciousness, or put in another way, there was a certain
communication between the two states, but also "a
certain incommunicability." (24) There was a "translucid
partition" between the two states which "opened when
Jesus wished to cross it." (25)

Far from all this being remote from the Christian
contemplative life, it is the very source and model for
it. "Through His infused prayer He experienced this
world; He entered with His consciousness, in order to
experience it in an ineffable manner, into this world
where He was alone with His Father and the Trinity...
And at the moment of the Agony and of the Passion He
can no longer enter there, He is barred from it by

uncrossable barriers, this is why He feels himself
abandoned. That has been the supreme exemplar of the
night of the spirit of the mystics, the absolutely complete
night. The whole world of the Vision and of the divinized
supraconscious was there, but He no longer experienced
it at all through His infused contemplation. And likewise
the radiance and the influx of this world on the entire
soul were more powerful than ever, but were no longer
seized at all by the consciousness, nor experienced." (26)

Here we are face-to-face with the foundation for
Maritain's remarks on the spiritual unconscious and
contemplative prayer, which we saw in **The Peasant of
the Garonne,** remarks which, as I noted, preceded the
writing of **The Peasant.**

Toward the end of this work on the humanity of Jesus
Maritain returns briefly to the question of Jesus' own
contemplative prayer. If there was a translucid partition
between the supra-conscious and the world of consciousness, then "nothing could **descend** in order to specify the
conscious activities; it is only general comfortings and
a participated light, in particular the light communicated
to the infused science, which descended into the world
of consciousness.

But with regard to the inverse movement, the
movement of **ascent** or of **ascension,** the translucid
partition was penetrable. As I said at the beginning,
through His infused contemplation Jesus entered, in order
to take there His repose and His joy, into the supra-
conscious paradise of His soul, where enraptured in union
with God His consciousness of viator approached almost
His Vision as comprehensor, and where He experienced
the divine things according to that savory experience of
love which the gifts of the Holy Spirit give, and which
in Christ-viator was incomparably higher than in any
other man, quite near, and more and more near, without
however attaining it, the point of unsurpassable perfection
(asymptotic) proper to Christ-comprehensor." (27)

By making this distinction between the two states of
Jesus' soul, Maritain opens a new way in which to see
Jesus not only as the model of complete and definitive
contemplation in terms of his supra-conscious, but also
a model for the contemplative life as it is actually
experienced by Christians in this life in light and

darkness.

The third and final book we have to examine is **Approches sans entraves,** the proofs of which were on their way to Maritain when he died. Again, our question is what scope did he give to the notion of the spiritual unconscious, and we find two important places where he made use of this idea, demonstrating how it had become a permanent part of his way of thinking.

In his essay, "Réflections sur la nature blessée," which comes under the heading, "Pour une épistémologie existentielle (I)," given as a seminar at Kolbsheim July 21, 1967, Maritain is extending St. Thomas' thought on the effects of original sin so that it will now embrace the working of the intellect, especially in its highest quests, like the intuition of being. In the state of original justice, reason, St. Thomas says, is elevated in perfection by God, and Maritain asks how this happens. It is not because grace perfects reason in its own nature, but "grace creates in the supra-conscious of the spirit a **heaven of the soul,** a supernatural heaven where grace itself rules - it is from this heaven of the soul that the theological virtues pass into consciousness (at least when they are developing normally) and by their radiance enlighten and fortify reason **in its** natural **exercise.**" (28)

It is no accident that this radiation of grace from the heaven of the soul follows closely the pattern of the grace in the heaven of the soul of Christ, influencing His world of consciousness. In the same essay Maritain attempts what he calls "a kind of transcendental psychology" by framing an explanation of how genuine metaphysical insight suffers from the impact of the disordered lower powers brought about by original sin. The normal and natural process of abstraction is marred by the imagination clinging to the idea so that our intelligences "unconsciously submitted to the vital pressure of the imagination." (29)

In a digression on the intuition of being he returns to some of the same thoughts he expressed in **The Peasant of the Garonne** on the location of the intuition of being in the spiritual unconscious. "The intellect, in the instant that the eye sees this rose and says: this rose is there, passes like a miracle - it is not a miracle, it is good fortune, a gift of nature suddenly received - to a superior level which is not only the third degree of abstraction, according to the language of the philosopher, but is also that of a moment of natural contemplation where thought is liberated from abstraction; and that is able to take place supraconsciously in the child, even before every abstractive operation, and more or less supra-consciously in the poet, as well as consciously in the apprentice philosopher or the philosopher in the process of meditation." (30)

Thus, in the course of this single essay Maritain uses the idea of the infraconscious to explain how metaphysical insights can fail to achieve their full stature, the supraconscious to explain a natural contemplation of the intuition of being, and the superconscious, this time as divinized by grace, to elucidate how the theological virtues effect reason.

In another essay, "Le Tenant-Lieu de théologie chez les simples, Pour une épistémologie existentielle (III)," given as a seminar to the Little Brothers on May 5th and 6th, 1969, Maritain is trying to clarify the process by which ordinary people receive inspirations from God. He feels that some of these inspirations come through the good offices of angels, and then he is left with the problem of just how the angels communicate with humans. St. Thomas says nothing about this question, and so Maritain, once again drawing on the modern psychological discovery of the unconscious, attempts to frame an answer. If we are open from below, as it were, to influences coming through the senses from material things - and for that matter, we could add, to influences coming from the infraconscious - why would it not be possible "to be open from on high - I mean in the supraconscious of the spirit - to the action exercised on it by a pure spirit?" (31)

Under the motion of God "the angel imprints on the supraconscious of the spirit an intellectual determination," "a simple spark of intelligibility in act, let us say an unformulated intuitive apprehension fecundating the intellect." And this seed is planted in the supraconscious "from where it passes into consciousness under the form of a mental word expressing an intuition." This is an idea that comes through "a knowledge by supraconscious instinct or connaturality." This idea is grasped by the

intellect by means of a light which is "the natural intuitivity of the spirit when the flash of a knowledge by
connaturality, too high and too pure to be consciously
seized, springs up in the superconscious before descending
into consciousness where it takes form in ideas or in
images, then in words." (32)

It is amply clear by now that by the end of Maritain's
life the notion of the spiritual unconscious had become
a powerful tool in his hands, which he employed with
great facility and good effect. But it is also an idea that
has such a potential range of application that he could
do no more than open the door to these depths of the
soul and hope there would be Thomists in the future who
would enter in and explore further. By way of conclusion,
to our examination of the three contemplations in the
previous chapters, we are now in a position to ask what
this future might hold by looking at each contemplation
in the light of the spiritual unconscious.

Maritain has made it clear that it is the intuition of
being that makes the metaphysician, and it is in striving
to penetrate into this mystery of being more vehemently
and profoundly that we can arrive at metaphysical
contemplation. He was the herald of the intuition of
being by not only grasping the primacy of esse, but
taking the next decisive step, as we have often seen in
the course of our analysis, of reflecting on the subjective
requirements of such an intuition. With his usual modesty
he refers to this remarkable achievement obliquely in
another of his break-through footnotes, this one coming
in his "Reflections on Wounded Nature."

"The intuition of being has been lived and practiced
by St. Thomas and the Thomists (the good Thomists), but
I do not know (perhaps due to my ignorance) of a treatise
or disquisitio where it has been explicitly studied by
them." (33)

But once we have grasped this revolutionary step that
Maritain has taken, we are carried by the very force of
his arguments to the brink of another vital break-through.
If the intuition of being is of such critical importance
for the whole metaphysical enterprise, then how can we
obtain it? How can we cultivate metaphysical contemplation? Maritain has insisted that the archsin of a Thomism
of the manuals and the classroom has been a notionalism

that stopped at essences and failed to see how they are the very faces and facets of esse. Essences can be transmitted in routine academic fashion, but how can an intuition, centered on existence, be passed on? Is this not the reason why the history of Thomism is the story of the discovery of the primacy of esse by St. Thomas and its loss by many Thomists over the ages? In the twentieth century this history has repeated itself again. With great effort the best minds of the Thomistic renaissance have rediscovered the central role of esse in Thomas' thought, but once again Thomism is in eclipse, and we have to ask whether this decline is related to its failure to discover ways in which to pass on its most important insight.

The whole trajectory of Maritain's metaphysical thought leads us to the question of how to obtain and transmit the intuition of being. But was Maritain, himself, aware of these implications? I think that he began to be towards the end of his life as he pondered his discovery that the intuition of being took place in the spiritual unconscious. In an open letter dated August 20, 1965 to two Polish lay Thomists, Jersy Kalinowsky and Stefan Swiezawski, he reflects on their book, La Philosophie à l'heure du concile:

"The misfortune of ordinary scholastic teaching, especially that of the manuals, has been to neglect in a practical way this essential intuitive element and replace it from the beginning by a pseudo-dialectic of concepts and formulas. There is nothing to do as long as the intellect has not **seen** - as long as the philosopher or apprentice philosopher has not had the intellectual intuition of being. It could be noted from this point of view the great pedagogical interest of a year of initiation to philosophy entirely centered on the need to lead spirits to the intuition of being and to the other fundamental intuitions by which Thomistic philosophy lives." (34)

We have traced the long road that Maritain followed in discovering the subjective requirements of the intuition of being, a road that finally ended at the spiritual unconscious, but if the spiritual unconscious is the very matrix in which the intuition of being is born, what conclusion must we draw from this? The intuition of being can never be simply a matter of words, for words have to do with the conceptual working of consciousness.

We are called not to some knowledge about, some theoretical appreciation of the mystery of being, but to enter into it and to say, as Maritain approvingly quotes from the authors of **La Philosophie à l'heure du concile**, "Je suis, à l'instar de saint Thomas, le contemplatif de l'être!" (35) I am, following the example of St. Thomas, a contemplative of being!

If we are to be contemplatives of being, this will involve not only recognizing that the philosophy of St. Thomas, which grew up within his theology, has to discover its own distinctive philosophical way of proceeding - as Maritain and other modern Thomists tried to do - but that it cannot follow the patterns of many modern philosophies that thrive for a moment with facile words, but wither rapidly away because they have not fully come to grips with the mystery of being. Such an attraction to the latest philosophical fashions would be fatal to a contemplation of being that demands a stillness of the mind, an active attentive listening, as Maritain puts it, that will allow us to hear the mystery of being that all things utter.

If we return to the passage in **The Peasant of the Garonne** where Maritain links the intuition of being with the spiritual unconscious, we will see that it leads us to the same conclusion. We must be receptive in our very depths to the I am, I exist, that each thing whispers. This means going beyond the level of concepts where essences are treated as essences and nothing more, and contacting the mystery of being that wells up from the very depths of the soul. The very existence of things, Maritain tells us, must sink into us so that "my awareness of it will strike me some day sharply enough (at times, violently) to stir and move my intellect up to that very world of preconscious activity, beyond any word or formula..." (36) Then once we have received this intuition in the depths of the spiritual unconscious, "if luck should take a hand, and if the eye of consciousness, sufficiently accustomed to the half-light, should penetrate a little, like a thief, this limbo of the preconscious, it can come about that this simple I am will seem like a revelation in the night..." (37) And those who are called to be metaphysicians can then reflect on this natural revelation of being and build their conceptual formulations firmly

upon it, and finally ponder it within themselves and arrive
at a penetrating metaphysical contemplation. If the
actual goal of metaphysics is this contemplation of being,
then the Thomism of the future must radically change
its way of proceeding in order to insure that the actual
transmission of metaphysical knowledge is centered on
this goal. This is not the place to try to indicate just
how such a transformed Thomistic metaphysics could
accomplish this purpose. It is enough, for now, to see
that if we are faithful to the inner direction of Maritain's work we are led to seriously consider such a
possibility, and see that it may be the only thing that
could break the circle of discovery and decline that has
plagued Thomism from its beginnings.

We will arrive at an equally revolutionary perspective
if we ponder the implications of Maritain's placing of
mystical contemplation in the spiritual unconscious.
Certainly, as we have seen, he was aware that this idea
had its historical antecedents, but even though there was
much talk in the past about the center of the soul, the
idea of a non-conscious dimension of the soul remained
implicit and in the background. So here is Maritain, again
opening up another door, this time for the future of
mystical theology.

One of the most intractable problems in the modern
history of spirituality has centered around the actual
experience and perceptibility of infused contemplation.
It was John of the Cross and Teresa of Avila who made
this problem much more acute and inescapable by
describing in detail the nature of contemplation and, in
St. John's case, the transitional stage from meditation
to contemplation. People after that time were compelled
to think about contemplation in a new way and ask themselves whether or not they were called to a life of
infused contemplation. We have seen how Maritain,
himself, was an assiduous reader of John of the Cross,
and how this reading might have influenced his thoughts
on a metaphysics of love. It would not be at all surprising if it effected his formulation of the notion of the
spiritual unconscious, as well. (38)

It would be possible to go through the writings of St.
John of the Cross and find many, many passages that
imply the existence of the spiritual unconscious, much in

the same fashion that St. Thomas, talking about the
agent intellect, implies it, as well. For example, in a
powerful passage in **The Ascent of Mount Carmel,** he
describes how it is possible for someone to receive a very
pure and strong infused contemplation without being
aware of it, just as a ray of light can penetrate a dark
room and be invisible unless it strikes the dust floating
in the air. The dust stands for the working of our conscious conceptual understanding, while the air represents
the depths of the soul, or in Maritain's language, the
supraconscious of the spirit divinized by grace. One way
to look at the controversies that sprang up in the wake
of the writings of the great Carmelite founders is to say
that they had to do with the question: Was it possible
for someone to actually be a contemplative and not
consciously realize the experience of contemplation?

These debates about the nature of contemplation filled
the 17th Century and did not subside until the crisis of
Quietism ushered in a decline in mystical studies that,
in some ways, lasted until the beginning of the 20th
Century. As soon as mystical theology came to life again
at the turn of the century, these same kinds of difficulties sprang up, and were being very much debated
when Maritain began his writings on mysticism in the
1920s.

But if we take Maritain's statement seriously that
contemplation takes place in the supraconscious, then it
immediately becomes evident that consciousness of
contemplation cannot be the essence of contemplation,
but rather, is an integral part of it. There is, of course,
no guarantee that an absence of awareness of the
contemplative experience is a sign that it exists in the
spiritual unconscious, but what Maritain's insight does do
is to give us a new way to look at these questions that
have accumulated over the centuries. When Maritain
writes about "contemplative prayer without apparent
graces," "where all the things described by St. John of
the Cross are divinely simplified" and "the soul is laid
bare and its very love-prayer as well - so arid at times
that it seems to fly into distraction and emptiness," we
are faced with a very important contemporary issue of
how people experience contemplation today that joins
hands with the former debates on the nature of contem-

plative experience. Surely Maritain is saying something more than St. John's constant refrain that contemplation is not to be confused with visions and revelations. But what does he really mean about the great things of John of the Cross divinely simplified, or how "the great signs that St. John of the Cross and Teresa of Avila have discerned do not appear?" It appears that he is referring to the conscious perception and awareness of these contemplative states, so carefully described by these Carmelite saints. If this is actually what he is doing, then he is setting the stage for a major reappraisal of the contemplative life that would have to steer a careful course between a facile equation of a lack of conscious experience of contemplation with contemplation, itself, and on the other hand, an identification of infused contemplation with the conscious, manifest and integral states described by St. John and St. Teresa.

By employing the idea of the spiritual unconscious, the mystical theologians of the future might find a way to make substantial progress in deepening our understanding of infused contemplation. Such an examination would have to make clear, as well, the Christocentric nature of contemplation which - building on Maritain's **On the Grace and Humanity of Jesus** - would elucidate how Jesus in His world of consciousness becomes the model for our own contemplative life. He enters into His divinized supraconscious and experiences infused prayer, but in His agony He suffers a dark night of the soul when His wayfarer consciousness is cut off from His supraconscious.

When we come to the question of natural mysticism there are two tasks that face the Maritain philosophers of the future. The first, as we saw in Chapter III, is to further develop the mysticism of the self in the light of the spiritual unconscious. If the way to reach an experience of natural mysticism is the leaving aside of all concepts, then this process, itself, points to a goal in the depths of the soul. And if this goal is an experience of the very existence of the soul and in and through it, God as the source of existence, albeit in a negative fashion, then where else can this pouring forth of existence take place but the very center of the spiritual unconscious,

which exists by receiving existence and exercising it as
its most intimate activity?

It is a keen understanding of the nature of the
mysticism of the self in the light of the spiritual unconscious which will be the instrument, par excellence, of
achieving the second task that faces the students of
Maritain's natural mysticism in the future. This is to try
to put the Christian side of dialogue with Eastern religions on a firmer foundation. Despite exceptions, some
of which we have already noted, it still remains true that
the promise of Maritain's work in this area remains
largely unrealized in the current dialogues with Hinduism
and Buddhism. It is Maritain's doctrine of the three
contemplations that can allow Christians to find a way
of drawing on the metaphysical and mystical riches of
their own tradition in their discussions with Eastern
religions. The three contemplations would allow them to
try to formulate in Christian terms what is the inner
nature of Hindu mystical experience, or Buddhist awakening.

An examination of why Christians engaged in dialogue
with Eastern religions have been slow to make use of the
riches of the metaphysics of St. Thomas and the mystical
tradition summed up so masterfully by St. John of the
Cross would lead us back to our first two considerations,
that is, the pedagogical sins of the Thomism of the past,
and the controversy that has surrounded understanding the
nature of infused contemplation ever since the time of
John of the Cross.

It is in the depths of the spiritual unconscious that
these three contemplations dwell, and while being distinct
in nature, interpenetrate each other. It is because of this
common matrix and close interrelationships that they
often generate similar vocabularies and can be confused
with each other. This is no more healthy than the opposite fault where, fearing confusion, we segregate each of
them in different parts of the soul as if they could have
nothing to do with each other. Maritain always insisted
that genuine distinctions, so vital for the life of the
intellect, have nothing to do with separations.

On the practical plane, his doctrine of the three
contemplations is a call for us to actually try to live
them out, and in this way, to see how closely and

intimately connected they are, and how much they can enrich each other. All of them center upon God. In metaphysical contemplation, it is God as the source of existence that all things make known to us if only we can fathom their deepest ontological natures. In the mysticism of the self it is God experienced as the very No-thing-ness that we come to at the heart of everything, and in mystical contemplation it is God in his infinite being who is calling us to loving union with Him. The future of Christian spirituality owes it to Maritain that it will be able to go down into the spiritual unconscious and enrich itself with a deeper understanding of these three contemplations.

NOTES

(1) The Peasant of the Garonne, p. 84.
(2) Ibid., p. 85.
(3) Ibid., p. 110.
(4) Ibid., p. 110-111.
(5) Ibid., p. 111.
(6) Ibid., p. 138.
(7) Ibid., p. 149.
(8) Ibid., p. 228.
(9) Ibid., p. 228, Note 103.
(10) Ibid., p. 230.
(11) Ibid., p. 235.
(12) Ibid., p. 234.
(13) Ibid.
(14) Ibid., p. 235.
(15) Ibid., p. 237.
(16) Ibid., p. 238.
(17) On the Grace and Humanity of Jesus, p. 7.
(18) Ibid., p. 47.
(19) Ibid., p. 49, Note 2.
(20) Ibid.
(21) Ibid., p. 55.
(22) Ibid.
(23) Ibid., p. 58.
(24) Ibid., p. 59.
(25) Ibid., p. 60.
(26) Ibid., p. 61.
(27) Ibid., p. 127.
(28) Approches sans entraves, p. 254.
(29) Ibid., p. 259.
(30) Ibid., p. 270.
(31) Ibid., p. 340.
(32) Ibid., p. 341, Note 34.
(33) Ibid., p. 267, Note 31.
(34) Ibid., p. 79.
(35) Ibid., p. 81.
(36) The Peasant of the Garonne, p. 138.
(37) Ibid.
(38) Charles A. Bernard suggests looking, as well, at medieval Augustinian mystical doctrine.

BIBLIOGRAPHY

I. Works by Jacques and Raissa Maritain:

Oeuvres complètes de Jacques et Raissa Maritain in 15 volumes. Editions Universitares Fribourg, Suisse, éditions Saint-Paul, Paris. The volumes are presented in chronological order.

The complete works will also be accompanied by a bibliography of Jacques and Raissa's writings. Preliminary versions of parts of it have been appearing as supplements to the Cahiers Jacques Maritain. Other extensive bibliographies of their works and works about them can be found in D. & I. Gallagher, The Achievement of Jacques and Raissa Maritain: A Bibliography, (1906-1961), New York, Doubleday, 1962. And in Laura Fraga de Almeida Sampaio's L'intuition dans la philosophie de Jacques Maritain, Paris, Libraire philosophique, 1963. For the works of Raissa Maritain see Judith Suther, Raissa Maritain: Pilgrim, Poet, Exile, New York, Fordham University Press, 1990.

La science moderne et la raison. Revue de Philosophie, Paris, 1910 (6), 575-603. Also in Antimoderne, 1922.

L'évolutionnisme de M. Bergson. Revue de Philosophie, Paris, 1911 (19) 467 ff. Also in: La Philosophie Bergsonienne, 1914.

Les deux Bergsonismes. Revue Thomiste, juillet-août, 1912, p. 433-450. Also in: La Philosophie Bergsonienne, 1914.

L'intuition. Au sens de connaissance instinctive ou d'inclination. Revue de

Philosophie, Paris, 1913 (23), p. 5-13. Also in La Philosophie Bergsonienne, 1914.

La philosophie Bergsonienne. Etudes critiques. Paris, Revière, 1914. 2nd edition, reviewed and augmented, 1930. 3rd edition, reviewed and augmented, Tèqui, 1948. Translation: Bergsonian Philosophy and Thomism. Translated by M.L. Andison in collaboration with J. Gordon Andison. New York, Philosophical Library, 1954.

Art et scolastique. Paris, Rouart, 1920. Translation: Art and Scholasticism. New York, Ch. Scribner's Sons, 1930.

Eléments de Philosophie. I. Introduction générale á la philosophie. Paris, Téqui, 1921. Translation: An Introduction to Philosophy, Translated by E.I. Watkin, Sheed & Ward, New York, 1930.

Préface: Driesch, H.: La philosophie de l'organisme. Paris, Marcel Rivière, 1921.

Théonas ou Les entretiens d'un sage et de deux philosophes sur diverses matières inégalement actuelles. Paris, Nouvelle Librairie Nationale, 1921. Translation: Théonas: Conversations of a Sage. Translated by F.J. Sheed. London & New York, Sheed & Ward, 1933.

Antimoderne. Paris, Ed. de la Revue des Jeunes, 1922.

De la vie d'oraison. En collaboration avec Maritain, R. Paris, St. Maurice, 1922, Rouart, 1924. Translation: Prayer and Intelligence, New York, Sheed & Ward, trans. A. Thorold, 1928.

Ernest Psichari. Revue Universelle, Paris, 1922. The same in Antimoderne, 1922.

Troisième cahier de Théonas: Connaissance de l'être. Revue Universelle, Paris, 1922, p. 109-18, 243-48, 655-64.

Pascal apologiste. Revue Hebdomadaire, 1923 (7). Also in: **Réflexions sur l'intelligence...,** 1924.

Une question sur la vie mystique et la contemplation. La vie spirituelle, mars 1923 (7), p. 636-50.

Réflexions sur l'intelligence et sur sa vie propre. Paris, Nouvelle Librairie Nationale, 1924.

Expérience mystique et philosophie. Revue de Philosophie, Paris, 1926 (33), p. 571-618.

Préface: Bruno de J.M.: **Saint Jean de la Croix.** Paris, Plon. 1929. Translation: **St. John of the Cross,** London, Sheed & Ward, 1932, pp. vii-xxvi.

Commentaire: Dandoy, G. **L'ontologie du Vedanta.** Essai sur l'acosmisme de l'advaita... Questions disputées, V. Paris, 1932, Desclée De Brouwer.

Distinguer pour unir ou les degrés du savoir. Paris, Desclée de Brouwer, 1932. Translation: **The Degrees of Knowledge,** New York, Charles Scribner's Sons, 1959.

De la philosophie chrétienne. Paris, 1933, Desclée de Brouwer. Translation: **An Essay in Christian Philosophy.** Translated by Flannery, E.H., Philosophical Lib., New York, 1955.

Sept leçons sur l'être et les premiers principes de la raison spéulative. Paris, Téqui, 1934. Translation: **A Preface to Metaphysics:** Seven Lectures on Being. New York, A Mentor Omega Book, 1962.

Science et sagesse. Paris, Labergerie, 1935. Translation: **Science and Wisdom,** translated by Wall, B. New York, Scribner's, 1940.

Freudisme et psychanalyse. Revue Thomiste, Paris, 1938 (44), p. 712-34. Also in: **Quatre essais sur l'esprit...,** 1939. Translation: in **Scholasticism and Politics,** New York, Image Books, 1960.

L'expérience mystique naturelle et le vide. Etudes Carmélitaines, Paris, 1938 (23, vol. 2), p. 116-39. Also in: Quatre essais sur l'esprit..., 1939. Translation: "The Natural Mystical Experience and the Void" in Understanding Mysticism, edited by Richard Woods. Garden City, New York: Image Books, 1980.

Situation de la poésie. Collection Courrier des Iles, 12. Paris, Desclée de Brouwer, 1938, 1947. In collaboration with Maritain, R. Translation: The Situation of Poetry. Translated by L. Marshall. New York, Philosophical Library, 1955.

Préface: Van der Meer de Walcheren, P.: Paradis Blanc, Paris, Desclée de Brouwer, 1939.

Quatre essais sur l'esprit dans sa condition charnelle. Paris, Desclée de Brouwer, 1939. Reviewed and augmented edition. Paris, Alsatia, 1956.

Scholasticism and Politics. Translation edited by Adler, M. New York, The Macmillan, 1940.

Les Grandes Amitiés: Souvenirs. New York: Maison Française, 1941. Repr. in one volume with Les Aventures de la grâce, double volume entitled Les Grandes Amitiés. Paris: Desclée de Brouwer, 1948. Translation: We Have Been Friends Together: Memoirs. Translated by Julie Kernan. New York and Toronto: Longmans, Green, 1942. English translation of combined volume: We Have Been Friends Together and Adventures in Grace: Memoirs. Trans. Julie Kernan. Garden City, NY: Doubleday Image Book, 1961.

La dialectique immanente du premier acte de Liberté. (Notes de Philosophie morale). Nova et Vetera, Freiburg, 1945 (20), p. 218-35. The same in: Raison et raisons, 1947. Translation: The Range of Reason, NY: Charles Scribner's Sons, 1942.

Court traité de l'existence et de l'existant. Paris, P. Hartmann, 1947. Translation: **Existence and the Existent,** NY: Image Books, 1956.

Préface: Bahya Ibn Pacuda: **Introduction aux devoirs des coeurs,** Paris: Desclée de Brouwer, 1950.

Approches de Dieu. Sagesse et cultures, Paris: Alsatia, 1953. Translation: **Approaches to God,** NY: Harper, 1954.

Creative Intuition in Art and Poetry. The A.W. Mellon lectures in the fine arts, National Gallery of Art. Washington, NY: Pantheon Books, 1953.

Sur la notion de la subsistence. Revue thomiste, 1954 (54), p. 242-56.

Preface: The Material Logic of John of St. Thomas: Basic Treatises. Translation. Chicago, IL: The Univ. of Chicago Press, 1955.

Liturgie et contemplation. Présence chrétienne. Bruges: Desclée de Brouwer, 1959. Translation: **Liturgy and Contemplation.** NY: Kenedy, 1960.

Journal de Raïssa. Ed. Jacques Maritain. Paris: Desclée de Brouwer, 1963. Translation: **Raïssa's Journal.** Albany, NY: Magi Books, 1974.

Carnet de Notes. Paris: Desclée de Brouwer, 1965. Translation: **Notebooks.** Albany, NY: Magi Books, 1984.

Le Paysan de la Garonne: Un vieux laïc s'interroge à propos du temps présent. Paris: Desclée de Brouwer, 1966. Translation: **The Peasant of the Garonne:** An Old Layman Questions Himself about the Present Time. NY: Holt, Rinehart and Winston, 1968.

De la grâce et de l'humanité de Jésus. Bruges: Desclée de Brouwer, 1967. Translation: **On the Grace and Humanity of Jesus.** NY: Herder and Herder, 1969.

De l'Eglise du Christ, O.C. Vol. XIII. Translation: **On the Church of Christ.** Univ. of Notre Dame Press.

Approches sans entraves, Paris: Fayard, 1973.

Marginalia by Jacques Maritain in **Quaestiones Disputatae** et Quaestiones
Duodecim Quodlibetales by S. Thomae Aquinatis, Volumen IV. Rome:
Typographia Pontificia, 1914. (Jacques Maritain Center, Notre Dame
University.)

Texts selected by Raïssa Maritain: **Textes Anciens:** Est-il pour nous "de
la plus grande utilité de connaître les grâces dont nous sommes favorisés"?
in Vie Spirituelle, Feb. 1925.

Les Dons du Saint-Esprit: Traité de Jean de Saint-Thomas. Trans. from
Latin to French by Raïssa Maritain. Juvisy: du Cerf, 1930.

A Propos de la Vocation des Petits Freres du Jesus by Jacques Maritain
in **Jacques Maritain:** Memorial pamphlet of the Little Brothers of Jesus,
1973?

"Trois lettres de Raïssa" in Cahiers Jacques Maritain, 7-8, Septembre
1983, p. 13-17

II. General Bibliography

Allion, Jean-Marie, "Le Cercle d'études Jacques et Raïssa Maritain et
l'édition des **Oeuvres complètes de Jacques et Raïssa Maritain**" in **Jacques
Maritain:** A Philosopher in the World, edited by J.L. Allard, Ottawa: Univ.
of Ottawa Press, 1985, p. 377-384

Arraj, James. **God, Zen and the Intuition of Being.** Chiloquin, OR: Inner
Growth Books, 1988.

Arraj, Tyra and James. The Man Who Loved Wisdom: The Story of Jacques Maritain. 70 Minute VHS Video. Chiloquin, OR: Inner Growth Videos, 1991.

Bars, Henri. Maritain et notre temps. Paris: Bernard Grasset Editeur, 1959.

Bars, Henry. A Maritain Bio-Bibliography. Edited and translated by Anthony O. Simon in Understanding Maritain: Philosopher and Friend, edited by Deal W. Hudson and Matthew J. Mancini, Macon, GA: Mercer University Press, 1987.

Bars, Henry. Untitled paper on mysticism, Jacques Maritain Center, University of Notre Dame, IN.

Berdyaev, Nicolas. Dream and Reality: An Essay in Autobiography. London: Geoffrey Bles, 1950.

Bergson, Henri. An Introduction to Metaphysics, translated by T.E. Hulme, NY: Putman's and Sons, 1912.

Bernard, Charles A. Le projet spirituel. Rome: Presses de l'Université Grégorienne, 1970.

Bernard, Charles A. "La mystique et les mystiques" in Gregorianum, 1967, Vol. 4, p. 766-775.

Bernard, Charles A. "La conscience mystique" in Studia Missionalia, 1977, Vol. 26, p. 87-115.

Brezik, Victor, B., ed. One Hundred Years of Thomism: Aeterni Patris and Afterwards a Symposium. Houston, TX: Center for Thomistic Studies, 1981.

Champagne, René. "Jacques Maritain, interprète de Jean de la Croix" in Jacques Maritain: A Philosopher in the World. Ottawa: University of Ottawa Press, 1985.

Doering, Bernard. Jacques **Maritain** and the French Catholic Intellectuals. Notre Dame, IN: Univ. of Notre Dame Press, 1983.

Etudes Carmélitaines. **Technique et contemplation.** Bruges: Desclée de Brouwer, 1949.

Floucat, Yves. **Vocation de l'homme et sagesse chrétienne.** Paris: Editions Saint-Paul, 1989.

Floucat, Yves. **Pour une philosophie chrétienne.** Paris: Téqui, 1981.

Floucat, Yves. "Presence de Jacques Maritain dans la penseé française actuelle et avenir de la sagesse chrétienne" in **La philosophie d'inspiration chrétienne en France.** Bruges: Desclée de Brouwer, 1988.

Fourest, Elisabeth. "Dernier salut à l'Amerique" in **Cahiers Jacques Maritain,** 4-5, p. 141-151.

Fowlie, W. **Jacob's Night:** The Religious Renascence in France. NY: Sheed and Ward, 1947.

Fowlie, W. "Remembering Jacques Maritain" in **The American Scholar,** 1988?, p. 355-366.

Galeazzi, G. "Il contributo teologico de J. Maritain: Indicazioni bibliografiche" in El **Contributo Teologico di Jacques Maritain,** Rome: LIbreria editrice Vaticana, 1984.

Gardeil, le Père A. **La structure de l'ame et l'expérience mystique.** Paris: Librairie Victor Lecoffre, 1927.

Gardet, Louis and Olivier Lacombe. **L'expérience du soi.** Paris: Desclée de Brouwer, 1981.

Gardet, Louis. **Thèmes et Textes Mystiques.** Paris: Alsatia, 1958.

Gardet, Louis. **Etudes de philosophie et de mystique comparées.** Paris: Librairie philosophique J. Vrin, 1972.

Gardet, Louis. "Recherches sur la "mystique naturelle"" in Jacques Maritain. Son oeuvre philosophique. In Revue thomiste, Paris: Desclée, 1948, p. 76ff.

Gardiner, Eveline. "Souvenirs sur mon oncle" in Cahiers Jacques Maritain, No. 2, p. 11-19.

Garrigou-Lagrange, R. "Prémystique naturelle et mystique surnaturelle" in Etudes Carmélitaines, 2, 1933, p. 51-77.

Garrigou-Lagrange, R. Perfection chrétienne et Contemplation selon St. Thomas d'Aquin et St. Jean de la Croix, 2 vols., Paris, 1923.

Gilson, E. Le Thomisme: Introduction a la philosophie de Saint Thomas d'Aquin. Paris: Librairie Philosophique J. Vrin, 1947.

Gilson, E. The Philosopher and the Theologian. NY: Random House, 1962.

Green, Julien and Jacques Maritain. Une Grande Amitié. Correspondance (1926-1972). Paris: Plon, 1979.

Griffin, John Howard and Yves R. Simon. Jacques Maritain: Homage in Words and Pictures. Albany, NY: Magi Books, Inc., 1974.

Grunelius, Antoinette. "Jacques Maritain et Kolbsheim" in Cahiers Jacques Maritain, 4-5, November 1982, p. 88-100.

Haenni, Marie-Thierry. "Contemplazione ed esperienza mistica nell'opera di Jacques Maritain" in Il contributo teologico di Jacques Maritain, Rome: Libreria Editrice Vaticana, 1984.

Hancock, Curtis L. "Maritain on Mystical Contemplation" in Understanding Maritain: Philosopher and Friend, edited by Deal W. Hudson and Matthew J. Mancini. Macon, GA: Mercer University Press, 1987, p. 257-288.

Hellman, John. "The Road to Vichy: Yves Simon's Lonely Protest Against Fascism" in Crisis, Vol. 6, No. 5, May 1988, p. 30-37.

Henle, R.J. et al., editors. **Conference-Seminar on Jacques Maritain's The Degrees of Knowledge.** St. Louis, MO: The American Maritain Association, 1981.

Jaki, Stanley L. "Maritain and Science" in **Understanding Maritain:** Philosopher and Friend. Edited by Deal W. Hudson and Matthew J. Mancini. Macon, GA: Mercer University Press, 1987.

John, Helen James. **The Thomist Spectrum.** NY: Fordham University Press, 1958.

Institut International "Jacques Maritain". "Olivier Lacombe" in **Notes et Documents,** Jan-March, 1980.

Iswolsky, Helen. **Light before Dusk:** A Russian Catholic in France, 1923-1941. NY: Longman's, Green and Co., 1942.

Kalinowski, Jerzy and Stefan Swiezawski. **La philosophie à l'heure du Concile.** Paris: Société d'Editions Internationales, 1965.

Kernan, Julie. **Our Friend, Jacques Maritain.** Garden City, NY: Doubleday & Co., 1975.

The Maritain-Merton Symposium. In **Cross Currents,** Vol. 31, No. 3, Fall, 1981.

McCool, G.A. "Jacques Maritain: A neo-thomist classic" in **The Journal of Religion,** No. 4, 1978, p. 380-404.

McInerny, Ralph. "Maritain's Intellectual and Spiritual Life: His Major Intuitions" in **Maritain:** A Philosopher in the World, edited by Jean-Louis Allard, Ottawa: University of Ottawa Press, 1985.

Merton-Maritain correspondence. 1949-1967. Unpublished. Maritain Archives, Kolbsheim.

Narcisse, Gilbert. "Le Père Labourdette lecteur de saint Jean de la Croix" in **Revue Thomiste,** Janvier-Mars 1992.

O'Meara, Thomas F. "Exploring the Depths. A Theological Tradition in Viewing the World Religions" in **In Verantwortung fur den Glauben,** Freiburg: Herder, 1992.

Papini, Roberto. "L'Institut international Jacques Maritain: les développements et le programme: l'héritage de Maritain" in **Jacques Maritain: A Philosopher in the World,** edited by Jean-Louis Allard. Ottawa: University of Ottawa Press, 1985.

Ravier, A., editor. **La mystique et les mystiques.** Desclée de Brouwer, 1965.

Rioux, Bertrand. "L'intuition de l'être chez Maritain" in **Jacques Maritain: The Man and His Metaphysics.** Mishawaka, IN: The American Maritain Association, 1988.

Bibliographie de Heinz (Schmitz) in **Cahiers Jacques Maritain,** No. 6.

Shook, Laurence. "Maritain and Gilson: Early Relations" in **Thomistic Papers II,** edited by L.A. Kennedy and J.C. Marler. Houston, TX: Center for Thomistic Studies, 1986.

Suther, Judith. **Raïssa Maritain:** Pilgrim, Poet, Exile. NY: Fordham University Press, 1990.

The Maritain Volume of the Thomist. Washington-NY: Sheed and Ward, 1943.

Trapani, John G. "Poetic Contemplation: An Undeveloped Aspect of Maritain's Epistomology" in **Jacques Maritain:** A Philosopher in the World. Ottawa: University of Ottawa Press, 1985.

Ward, Leo R. "Meeting Jacques Maritain" in The Review of Politics, Vol. 44, No. 4, October, 1982.

Williams, Brooke. "Mystical Contemplation in the Thought of Yves R. Simon and Jacques Maritain" in Notes et Documents, No. 14, Jan.-Mar. 1979.

INNER GROWTH BOOKS AND VIDEOS

CHRISTIAN METAPHYSICS

THE MAN WHO LOVED WISDOM: The Story of Jacques Maritain. 70 Minutes, VHS Video, $30

This is a unique documentary of one of modern Catholicism's most creative philosophers. It traces the lives and work of Jacques Maritain (1882-1973), his wife Raissa and her sister Vera through rare photos, interviews with people who knew them, and location shots.

Meet Louis Chamming's, a Parisian philosopher and disciple of Maritain, and his wife, Soizick, Olivier Lacombe, the noted Indologist and friend of Maritain, and many other friends, old and new: Anthony Simon, Cornelia Borgerhoff, Joseph and Irene Lynch, Roberto Papini, Deal Hudson, Ralph McInerny, René Mougel, and Antoinette Grunelius. And visit the Latin Quarter and Montmartre in Paris, Heidelberg, New York, Rome, Princeton and Kolbsheim to see where the Maritains lived out their lives.

This is a fine introduction for those who have not yet met Maritain, and a beautiful chance to remember for his many friends.

A TASTE OF EXISTENCE: An Interview with W. Norris Clarke, S.J. on the Metaphysics of St. Thomas Aquinas. 82 Minute VHS Video, $20. Audiotape from Video: $6

What does metaphysics have to do with everyday life? What happens when a New York cab driver fantasizes about winning the lottery? What special feeling transpires when a dying unwed mother gives birth? And what does a teenager stuck high on a cliff discover about "a taste of existence"?

Fr. Clarke speaks clearly about the metaphysics of St. Thomas, but instead of this subject being bookish and boring, the viewer will become engrossed in facing the deep questions of what is real, what is meaningful, and what is true that lie in the depths of each of us. His personal enthusiasm is evident as he takes us through his own stages of discovery and love of St. Thomas' metaphysics, and he gives excellent suggestions of how we, too, can begin our own journey into metaphysics.

Fr. Clarke has been the president of the American Catholic Philosophical Association and the winner of its Aquinas medal, and co-founder and editor of the International Philosophical Quarterly, has taught for many years at Fordham University, and has lectured around the country. He tackles questions like what is metaphysics, the real life experiences that are its foundation, the discovery of an existential Thomism in the 20th century, the relationship between essence and existence, the nature of matter, and more.

BUDDHIST-CHRISTIAN DIALOGUE

BLOSSOMS OF SILENCE: A Visit with Jim Grob. 66 Minute VHS Video, $20. Audiotape from video: $6

East meets West in the inner adventures of Jim Grob. Years of formal discursive Christian meditation had led him to an apparent dead-end in the life of prayer. Then much later he discovered the interior silence that is at the heart of Zen. Silent sitting led to a series of numinous dreams, awakening experiences, Christian contemplative experiences, and finally an understanding of the necessity of going by faith.

Here is one of the clearest explanations of the relationship of Zen enlightenment to Christian mystical experiences from a practitioner of both paths. Format: Straight interview punctuated by Jim Grob reading his haiku, which are like blossoms of silence.

BUDDHIST-CHRISTIAN DIALOGUE IN ACTION: Highlights of the Working Group "Zen Awakening and Christian Contemplation: Practice in Both Traditions" held at the 4th International Buddhist-Christian Dialogue Conference, Boston University July 30-Aug. 3, 1992. 100 Minute VHS Video, $20. Audiotape: $6

Nine people active in the Buddhist Christian dialogue speak from the heart about their own inner journeys: Ruben Habito, one of the first Catholics to have Kensho confirmed by a Japanese master; Patricia Dai-en Bennage, a Soto Zen priest and first foreigner/woman to complete full advanced teacher training; Susan Ji-on Postal, a Zen priest and leader of the Meeting House Zen Group in Rye, New York; Astrid O'Brien, Associate Professor of Philosophy at Fordham University; Robert Kennedy, a Jesuit priest recently installed as a Zen teacher by Tetsugen Glassman; Thomas Hand, a Jesuit priest and pioneer of Zen-Christian dialogue in Japan; Sr. Agnes Lee, a Chinese Catholic nun and Zen practitioner; Jim and Tyra Arraj.

Also included are some responses from the audience.

ZEN JOURNEY: A Visit with Susan Postal. 99 Minute VHS Video, $25

Susan Jion Postal, ordained Zen Priest and student of the late Maurine Stuart, Roshi of the Cambridge Buddhist Assoc., has been studying and practicing in the Buddhist tradition for more than 20 years. Beginning with Dzogchen practice in the Tibetan Vajrayana, she did Soto Zen study at the Zen Community of New York and then Rinzai based Zen practice in Cambridge. Susan, the mother of two grown children, works in a nursing home in Therapeutic Recreation, and she is the leader of the Meeting House Zen Group in Rye, New York.

Format: the video alternates between Susan's touching account of her inner Zen journey and beautiful scenes of Zen practice, including chanting, a tea ceremony, basic sitting instructions, and a formal Dharma talk.

GOD, ZEN AND THE INTUITION OF BEING by James Arraj. 144pp, paper, $11

An encounter between Zen, the metaphysics of St. Thomas, and the mysticism of John of the Cross is inevitable. But the success of this meeting depends on how deeply we grasp their inner natures, and how much we thirst for the great gifts that each participant has to offer.

PART I explores the intuition of being, the metaphysical heart of Thomism, which it has neglected to its own great peril. It sees the metaphysics of St. Thomas through the eyes of one of his greatest 20th century followers, Jacques Maritain. It asks the questions, "Why does the Thomistic renewal seem to be over?" "And why did St. Thomas have to be rediscovered to begin with?" And it answers that Thomism has neglected its distinctive form of metaphysical insight, the intuition of being. Further, Thomism has yet to really ask how to cultivate this metaphysical seeing.

PART II examines how the spirit of Zen can reanimate Thomistic metaphysics and in its turn understand its own nature better by seeing how the metaphysics of St. Thomas views it. It is the metaphysics of St. Thomas that is the least known and potentially one of the most powerful partners in any Zen-Christian or Buddhist-Christian dialogue. It looks at Zen as metaphysical insight, drawing on the work of Keiji Nishitani, Katsuki Sekida and Toshihijo Izutsu.

PART III attempts to situate Zen between metaphysics and Christian mysticism, and describes Zen as a metaphysical mysticism, or even a mystical metaphysics, and it brings it into relationship with the mysticism of John of the Cross and the issue of acquired contemplation, and addresses the issue of whether there can be a Zen Catholicism.

"...*An engagingly earnest exploration of the scholastic metaphysics of medieval Thomas Aquinas and its modern revival (neo-Thomism) through Jacques Maritain, the Christian existentialist (part 1) and an examination of Zen and the experience of satori in an equally thorough manner (part 2) leads Arraj to the quite legitimate insight that comparison and contrast of Thomistic "intuition of being" with Zen experience do indeed present areas for dialogue and conversation (part 3).*" Buddhist-Christian Studies, Vol. 10, 1990*

"...*presents us with an interesting and acute vision of the relationships between Thomist metaphysics, the enlightenment of Zen and the Catholic mysticism centered on the two reformers of Carmel, but more expressly on St. John of the Cross... The book is a very worthy contribution to the studies of comparative mysticism and a validation of the mystical soul of Thomist metaphysics, and its value in the actual Christian-Eastern dialogue.*" Revista de Espiritualidad, 49 (1990)*

"...*a challenging book for those interested in points of contact between Zen and Christianity... recommended for public and private libraries and for theological collections.*" En Christo Book Reviews*

CHRISTIAN CONTEMPLATION AND ZEN ENLIGHTENMENT: Are They the Same? A Workshop with James Arraj. 4 Hours, VHS Video, $25. Audiotape from video: $12

This is a workshop given in August, 1991 at the Spiritual Life Center in Wichita, Kansas. It describes how Zen is coming into the Catholic Church, especially through the Catholic students of the late Zen master, Koun Yamada, and it tries to give the flavor of Zen practice by including part of an actual Zen awakening account (excerpted from **Zen Journey,** above). Then it compares Zen enlightenment with Christian metaphysics and mystical experience by looking at contemplation, according to John of the Cross, including the story of a Christian contemplative experience (excerpted from **A Contemplative Journey,** see below) and the revolutionary insight to be found in the metaphysics of Thomas Aquinas. Finally, it frames an explanation of Zen enlightenment from a Christian point of view, following the work of Jacques Maritain on the mysticism of the Self.

HINDU-CHRISTIAN DIALOGUE

EXPLORING THE CHRISTIAN-HINDU DIALOGUE: A Visit with Bede Griffiths and Russill Paul. 55 Minute VHS Video, $20. Audiotape from video: $6

Bede Griffiths is a Benedictine monk, a pioneer of the Christian-Hindu dialogue, and the head of Shantivanam, a Christian ashram in India. Here he discusses his life in India, his attempts to enrich the Christian contemplative path through Hindu mysticism, and his hope for the formation of small lay contemplative communities in the West.

Russill Paul is a friend and disciple of Bede Griffiths, and a professional musician. Born in the Anglo-Indian community of Madras in southern India, he has spent years living at Shantivanam. He is creating a new form of music whose goal is to aid the contemplative life, and exploring the possibility of creating lay contemplative communities in the United States. He briefly describes his life and work, and gives an example of his new form of music. Format: straight interviews with a musical selection by Russill Paul.

CHRISTIAN PRAYER AND KUNDALINI: A Visit with Philip St. Romain. 90 Minute VHS Video, $20. Audiotape from video: $6

After years devoted to the Christian life of prayer Philip St. Romain experienced an unanticipated awakening of an energy that in ancient India was called Kundalini or serpent power, and which played an important role in Hindu mystical experience. He unwittingly became a laboratory in which Christian spirituality meets the wisdom of the East. This is a detailed account of both his Christian life and his Kundalini awakening.

Philip is the associate director for lay leadership and development at the Spiritual Life Center, Wichita, Kansas where he helps direct a wide variety of programs, as well as give retreats and workshops.

Format: Straight interview with some introductory shots of Philip at home, and later at the Spiritual Life Center.

KUNDALINI ENERGY AND CHRISTIAN SPIRITUALITY: A Workshop with Philip St. Romain. 2 Hour VHS Video, $20 Audiotape from video: $6

This workshop builds on Philip's story told in the 90 Minute video, "Christian Prayer and Kundalini" (listed above), and explores the meaning of Kundalini and its relationship to Christian spirituality. This workshop was videotaped live at a conference given in August, 1991 at the Spiritual Life Institute in Wichita, Kansas.

THE HEART OF THE CHRISTIAN-HINDU DIALOGUE: A Conversation with Wayne Teasdale. 84 Minute VHS Video, $20 Audiotape from Video: $6

Wayne Teasdale is a Christian sannyasi who follows both the Christian and Hindu contemplative paths. He is a friend and disciple of Bede Griffiths, a Benedictine monk who heads Shantivanam, a Christian-Hindu ashram in India. This wide-ranging interview, taped at Hundred Acres Monastery in New Hampshire, describes the history of the Christian-Hindu dialogue in India, the work of Bede Griffiths, and tackles the difficult question of the relationship between Hindu and Christian mystical experience.

Format: straight interview with several insertions of photographs taken at Shantivanam.

CHRISTIAN SPIRITUALITY AND MYSTICISM

A CENTERING PRAYER RETREAT with Fr. M. Basil
Pennington, O.C.S.O. 3 Hours, 2 VHS Videocassettes, $25
Audiotapes from Videos: $12

This is a complete centering prayer retreat ideal for both
individual or group use. Centering prayer is a very simple way
of praying by making use of a prayer word. This retreat was
videotaped live at a retreat given in August, 1991 at the
Spiritual Life Center, Wichita, Kansas. It presents a detailed
explanation of how to practice centering prayer, and includes
advice, stories and warm good humor as Fr. Pennington
encourages the retreatants to make centering prayer an
important part of their daily life.

Fr. Basil is one of centering prayer's pioneering presenters,
a Trappist monk, and the author of many books on prayer and
monasticism.

CHRISTIAN SPIRITUALITY TODAY AND TOMORROW. 90
Minute VHS Video, $15. Audiotape from Video: $6

Explores what is happening in the field of Christian spirituality in the U.S. today and what development might be on the
horizon by means of interviews with men and women who work
in the field: visit with Tom Santa, the director of the new
Spiritual Life Center in Wichita, Kansas, and tour one of the
country's most carefully planned retreat facilities. And in a
series of interviews taped at the Spiritual Life Center meet
Margaret Goldsbury of Our Lady of Peace Spiritual Life Center
in Rhode Island, Patrick Eastman, director of spirituality for the
Diocese of Tulsa, and Jane Comerford, director of Still Point,
Seattle, Washington.

The video concludes with an overview on the present state,
and future possibilities of Christian spirituality given by James
Arraj at the Spiritual Life Center, August 1991.

A CONTEMPLATIVE JOURNEY: An Interview with Joseph
Patchett on Christian Mysticism. 90 Minute VHS Video, $20
Audiotape from Video: $6

When Joseph Patchett speaks about contemplation and St.
John of the Cross it is like a breath of fresh air. He is direct
and down to earth as he recounts his own remarkable conversion, sparked by a car accident and the writings of an Indian
yogi that gave him a taste of mystical experience, and set him
on the road to try to live the contemplative life, and this is
something he is still trying to do today as a married man with
six children and a normal job, and as a Third Order Carmelite.

This is an inspiring story and a penetrating commentary on
John of the Cross who appears, not as the exponent of some
exotic theory, but as a practical guide for those called to the
experience of union with God which St. John called infused
contemplation.

ARE THERE REALLY CONTEMPLATIVES TODAY? by James Arraj. 60 Minute audiotape, $6

A careful exploration of some of the important questions that surround today's interest in contemplation, or Christian mystical experience. It touches on the many ways the word contemplation is used today, and examines what it means for St. John of the Cross, and tackles the difficult issues of the dark night of sense and whether people today experience St. John's infused contemplation.

ST. JOHN OF THE CROSS AND DR. C.G. JUNG: Christian Mysticism in the light of Jungian Psychology by James Arraj. 208pp, paper, $12

"Many current attempts to revitalize the life of prayer are inspired by either the writings of St. John of the Cross or the psychology of Dr. C.G. Jung. Both are excellent choices. Even better would be a program of renewal under their joint inspiration. Yet such a program faces three serious challenges: theological misgivings about the compatibility of Jung's psychology with Christian belief, long-standing misinterpretations of St. John's doctrine on contemplation, and the need to clarify the relationship between Jung's process of individuation and contemplation. Parts I and II are devoted to resolving these first two problems, while Part III gives a practical demonstration of the relationship between individuation and contemplation in St. John's life and in a variety of contemporary spiritual problems." From the Introduction

"The story of Jung's encounter with Fr. Victor White suggests the difficulties of a task which nevertheless must be carried out: the collaboration of psychology and theology...very complete bibliography." Choice

"This book deserves to be read. It is well written, well documented, easy to follow, and on occasion fascinating..." Spirituality Today

"Arraj has presented both Jung and John of the Cross in a competent manner. He related the two figures in a deeply thoughtful way, and challenges the reader to reflect along with him..." John Welch. O.C.D., author of Spiritual Pilgrims: Carl Jung and Teresa of Avila, in Carmelus

JUNGIAN-CHRISTIAN DIALOGUE

JUNGIAN PSYCHOLOGY AND SPIRITUAL DIRECTION: A Visit with Don Bisson. 53 Minute VHS Video, $20. Audiotape from video: $6

Don Bisson is a Marist Brother and a pioneer in exploring the deeper levels of the Jungian-Christian dialogue. Out of his own experience of Jungian analysis and the inadequacies of traditional spiritual direction, he has created a new form of spiritual direction that integrates Jung's process of individuation with the quest for a deeper life of prayer, and he has refined this kind of spiritual direction in his work with members of the inner city parish in Oakland, California, where he lives.

In **Jungian Psychology and Spiritual Direction** he explains the nature of this kind of spiritual direction, illustrates it with case studies, and sets it within the larger context of the Jungian-- Christian dialogue. Format: straight interview.

JUNGIAN AND CATHOLIC? The Promises and Problems of the Jungian-Christian Dialogue by James Arraj. 128pp, paper, $10

JUNGIAN AND CATHOLIC? continues along the path opened by **St. John of the Cross and Dr. C.G. Jung.** But instead of focusing on Christian spirituality, it explores how Christian philosophers and theologians could enter into a deeper dialogue with Jungian psychologists.

PART I examines the basic positions that have emerged during the course of the discussions and debates between Jung's psychology and Christianity. They range from an identification of the Christian life with Jung's archetypes and the process of individuation to an outright rejection of his psychology as a threat to it. In contrast to these extremes a genuinely interactive approach holds the most promise for the future.

PART II looks at the relationship between Jung's psychology and the philosophical psychology of Thomas Aquinas.

PART III examines the impact that Jungian psychology could have on a theology smart enough not to accept Jung's comments on the Trinity as theology, but daring enough to use his psychology to explore how revelation is effected by being received into an archetypically conditioned psyche.

PART IV touches on how Jung's psychology could meet the great need the Church has for a viable empirical psychology which could be employed in the field of Christian spirituality.

CHRISTIAN THEOLOGY & MORALITY

STRAIGHT TALK: Teenagers and Sex. 43 Minute VHS Video, $20

Fr. Bernard Sander, O.S.B., of Mount Angel Abbey, Oregon, had long been concerned about the serious problems he found among young people caused by premarital sexual activity, and so he decided to do something about it. He invited four teenagers, an unwed mother, a gynecologist, a urologist, a psychiatrist, and a moral theologian to spend a day at the Abbey frankly discussing this issue.

The result of an honest and forceful video that looks at:
* the pressures teenagers feel to become sexually active
* the pain of an unexpected pregnancy
* the medical consequences of today's widespread sexual activity among teens

* the psychological problems that result from abortion and adoption

* a Christian understanding of sexuality

STRAIGHT TALK has been made with the help of teenagers for teenagers, and for those who care the most about them. It is a compassionate but clear presentation of the problems that our teenagers face seen against the background of Christian values.

This is a video that will ignite discussion among teenagers about these critical issues, and encourage them to resist the pressures they are under. It is ideal for youth groups, classrooms, and parents who want a way to enter into deeper discussion of these issues with their children.

THE INNER NATURE OF FAITH: A Mysterious Knowledge Coming Through the Heart by James Arraj. 144pp, paper, $10

Faith is a highly distinctive kind of knowledge, a knowledge that works through love, through the heart, and because we misunderstand the nature of this knowledge we resist it, or fail to respond fully to its mysterious call.

A penetrating theological study of the nature of faith under the aspect of what St. Thomas Aquinas called knowledge by connaturality, which is a knowledge that works through love. Starting from the experience of human love, it explores how this notion of connaturality is being slowly rediscovered in the 20th century, and is firmly rooted in the Scriptures and Fathers and the philosophy of Jacques Maritain. Then it goes on to examine the act of faith, the nature of theology, and mysticism in the light of this knowledge coming through love.

IS THERE A SOLUTION TO THE CATHOLIC DEBATE ON CONTRACEPTION? by James Arraj. 128pp, paper, $9

More than twenty years after Pope Paul VI's encyclical **Humanae Vitae**, contraception remains a deeply divisive problem in the Catholic Church. It absorbs energy that could be applied to other pressing issues, and it alienates Catholics from the life of their Church.

Is there a solution to the question of contraception? Is a reconciliation possible between the two sides of the debate? This book proposes such a solution. This would be a presumptuous undertaking except for the fact that many of the elements for a solution already exist, and what is needed is a way to bring them all together.

ABOUT THE AUTHOR

Jim Arraj lives with his wife, Tyra, deep in a forest far from paved roads and power lines near Crater Lake, Oregon. There they built their own house, grow salads in a solar greenhouse, and create books and videos.

Jim has a doctorate in theology from the Gregorian University in Rome, and they both have travelled widely to do research and meet pioneers in the new encounter among Christian metaphysics and mysticism, Jungian psychology, Eastern religions, and a new sense of the earth.

ORDER FORM

Qty.	Title	Price each

Postage: $1.50 for first item
50¢ for each add'l item.
Foreign: $2.00 for first item
$1 for each add'l item.

Subtotal _____

Shipping _____

Total _____

Here is my check payable to: *INNER GROWTH BOOKS & VIDEOS*
 Box 520, Chiloquin, OR 97624   (503) 783-3126

Name _____

Address _____

City, State, Zip _____